HOW THEY CHOKED

For Jennie Georgia Bragg
—G. B.

First published in the United States of America in May 2014
by Walker Books for Young Readers, an imprint of Bloomsbury Publishing, Inc.
Paperback edition first published in June 2016 by Bloomsbury Children's Books
www.bloomsbury.com

Bloomsbury is a registered trademark of Bloomsbury Publishing Plc

For information about permission to reproduce selections from this book, write to
Permissions, Bloomsbury Children's Books, 1385 Broadway, New York, New York 10018
Bloomsbury books may be purchased for business or promotional use. For information on bulk purchases please
contact Macmillan Corporate and Premium Sales Department at specialmarkets@macmillan.com

The Library of Congress has cataloged the hardcover edition as follows:
Bragg, Georgia.
How they choked : failures, flops, and flaws of the awfully famous /
by Georgia Bragg ; illustrated by Kevin O'Malley.
pages   cm
ISBN 978-0-8027-3488-4 (hardcover) • ISBN 978-0-8027-3489-I (reinforced)
I. History—Errors, inventions, etc.—Juvenile literature. 2. Celebrities—Conduct of life—Juvenile literature.
3. Decision making—Juvenile literature. I. O'Malley, Kevin, illustrator. II. Title.
CT105.B724 2014   920—dc23   2013039127

ISBN 978-1-68119-216-1 (paperback)

Art created with Black Micron 005 by Pigma on layout paper
Typeset in Centaur
Printed in China by C&C Offset Printing Co., Ltd., Shenzhen, Guangdong
7 9 10 8 6

HOW THEY CHOKED

FAILURES, FLOPS, AND FLAWS OF THE AWFULLY FAMOUS

GEORGIA BRAGG

ILLUSTRATED BY KEVIN O'MALLEY

BLOOMSBURY

NEW YORK LONDON OXFORD NEW DELHI SYDNEY

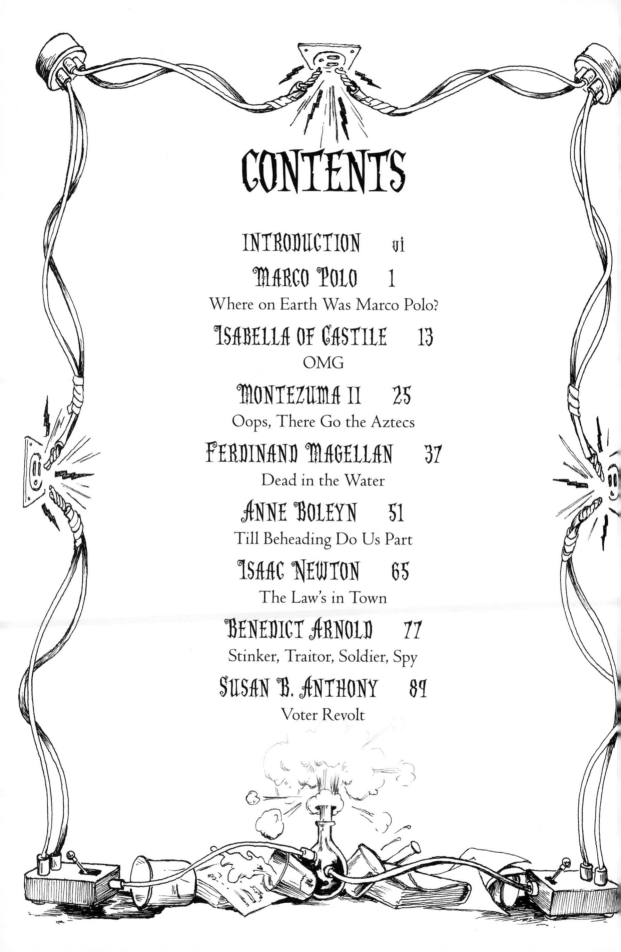

CONTENTS

INTRODUCTION

WARNING:
Nobody's Perfect;
Get Used to It

IF YOU ONLY want to see people at their best, this book isn't for you.

I've been asked, "Don't you ever write anything with a happy ending?" So far, no, and not in this book either. It's full of bad news about how some of the world's most successful people failed, flunked, choked, or blew it. What's not to love? There's *nothing better* than reading about how someone else messed up.

Juicy failures don't often make it into biographies because sometimes historians lose sight of the fact that their subjects were human beings. Real people make mistakes (even historians). Nobody's perfect—not your parents, your teachers, or even you.

Neither was the genius who figured out gravity and then abandoned science to make gold. There was also the famous pilot who never read the instruction manual, the cheating baseball slugger, and the war hero turned spy. And let's not forget the torture-loving queen and the famous artist who couldn't sell a painting.

The best among them learned from their failure, but for the most part this book is full of renowned overachievers, brave show-offs, and brilliant boneheads.

It's time to stop sweeping these monumental belly flops under the rug and off websites, and to get them back into the world's memory drive, because as long as we're human, failure is here to stay.

So buckle up, and don't go idolizing people before you know everything about them. You may be in for some surprises on this ride.

MARCO POLO

WHERE ON EARTH WAS MARCO POLO?

Adventurer
Born: Venice, Italy,
1254
Died: Venice, Italy,
January 8, 1324
70 years old

MARCO? POLO!

Marco? Polo!

Marco?

Exactly. Where was Marco Polo? Just like in the game of tag that's been played about a million times, the *real* Marco Polo was a master escape artist. While earning frequent-camel miles in the Far East, he almost suffocated in a sandstorm, battled crocodiles, and dodged cannibals. Those are people who eat other people, and

1

especially tasty are the ones they kill themselves. While running around so no one would eat him, Marco's own dad gave him away to the most dangerous man on earth. Marco Polo survived close calls all over the map, only to make the biggest mistake of his life a few miles from home. But if ever there was a guy who could turn a narrow escape into a good story, it was Marco Polo. He just had to write it down.

In 1254, the year Marco Polo was born in Venice, Italy, his traveling-salesman father was already off on the medieval version of a road trip, meaning he was on foot, lugging his stuff on his back. Throughout Europe, there was a growing demand for silk, spices, and gunpowder, which could only be found on the continent of Asia, and his dad went to get some. While Dad was off looking for good deals, Marco's mom died. Since no one knew when, or if, his dad would be back, Marco was treated like an orphan and raised by relatives. All plans of a welcome-home party for Dad were put to rest as the years rolled by, but one day, out of the blue, Marco's travel-worn dad showed up in Venice with bolts of silk, expensive jewels sewn into his clothes, and in dire need of a bath. Marco was fifteen years old when father and son saw each other for the first time.

Marco hung on his father's every word as he explained that he hadn't been on just any old sales trip. He had met Kublai Khan, ruler

of the Mongol Empire, which encompassed one-fifth of all the land on Earth. Khan had killed more people in more places than any other man of his time. A person did what Khan wanted, and he had ordered Marco's dad to bring him a response to his personal note to the pope requesting one hundred wise men and oil from the Holy Sepulchre in Jerusalem, where Jesus was buried. Dad asked Marco to help with his mission.

Marco had no intention of letting his dad down (or out of his sight). He wanted to be a worthy son, so at seventeen years old, having never been beyond the canals of Venice, Marco joined his dad and an uncle on the journey. They got the oil, and the pope's note that Khan wanted, which was harder than it sounds. But they didn't bother bringing any wise men. The Polos headed east to China, and the palace of Kublai Khan, thousands of miles away.

The only route to the Far East was the Silk Road, which was the first import/export superhighway, except this was before trains,

planes, and automobiles. It wasn't paved, and there were no signs. The Silk Road was not for sissies. The only reason it was called "silk" anything was because silk was what you could buy for cheap if you survived the journey, but calling it a "road" was wishful thinking. If anything, it was many dirt paths crisscrossing Asia and Africa. It wound its way eastward through the boiling Gobi Desert, up freezing Mount Ararat, and across fourteen-thousand-foot-high grasslands—inhospitable places without fresh water or food. Miles of ocean routes were part of the Silk *Road* too. On land and sea, thieves were everywhere, the locals fought each other, and there was no such thing as a water bottle, thermal underwear, or hiking boots. It took more than a good sense of direction to figure out the jumble of pathways: it took guts and perseverance. No one had to be good at reading a map because there wasn't one. It was possible to catch a ride on an ox, a camel, or a boat, but mostly travelers put one foot in front of the other for thousands of miles.

The endless campout gave the long-lost father and son a chance for some quality time getting to know each other over many bowls of sheep soup. Marco made sure his father would be proud of him, and instinctually, Marco knew how to behave so they wouldn't all get murdered by wandering nomads. He was tough, chatty, and adaptable. Marco was also friendly, open-minded, and charming—appealing qualities that don't need translation no matter what the native language. Marco blossomed during the road trip; he wasn't sword-happy, he had no religious agenda, and his free-to-be-you-and-me attitude was infectious. It took over three years to go the 4,900 miles from Venice, Italy, to Cambulac, China, which is current-day Beijing.

Marco was about twenty years old when they arrived at the palace of Kublai Khan. He was wowed by the huge, square royal city, the statues of two-headed dragons, and the palace full of Chinese furniture. So they wouldn't soil the embroidered rugs, the Polos put white slippers over their globe-trotting feet before meeting the emperor. The royal Kublai Khan wore an eyeful of silk. Jade and pearls were woven into the layers, tastefully set off against his red silk leggings.

Marco's dad introduced him to the man under the mountain of silk: "Sir, he is my son and your man, whom as the dearest thing I had in this world I have brought with great peril and ado from such distant lands to present him to thee for thy servant."

Instead of delivering the requested wise men, Marco's dad *handed him over* to the flighty, power-hungry ruler with a warrior mentality. Was he being punished? One false move and Marco would be dead, like the thousands of other people Kublai had executed on a whim.

Had Marco disappointed his father so much that he'd leave him with a killer?

His father and uncle were allowed to lounge around the palace as honored guests from the West, while Marco was at the mercy of mud-smeared soothsayers guiding Khan's every move.

Whatever survival skills Marco had, he was going to need them. The father-son bonding-and-sightseeing trip was definitely over. Marco was on his own.

Kublai put Marco right back on the road. Most of Kublai's staff were fighters, destroying any hint of revolt within his conquered empire. Since anyone could see Marco wasn't the fighter type, Kublai commanded Marco to collect taxes for him. That was dangerous too. A stranger bopping into town demanding money was an easy target for murder—especially if he was a Westerner.

Because his life depended on it, Marco Polo knocked himself out learning Mongolian, Persian, and a couple of other languages he needed to know to survive. Periodically, he'd return to Kublai Khan and hand over the tax money. Out of touch with his sprawling kingdom, Kublai interrogated Marco about the latest news. If Marco didn't share a lot of juicy gossip, Khan would rage and come unglued, so Marco mastered blabby storytelling, elaborating and puffing up details. Every time he had an audience with Khan, it was like the death-elimination round of *The Mongolian Empire's Got Talent*. This went on for seventeen years.

Marco wanted to go home. His father and uncle were ready to go too; they hadn't left, because war broke out along the route. Now they were old and they needed Marco's help getting back to Venice. Marco didn't owe his dad a thing after what he had done to him, but he agreed to help him anyway. After begging, and lying about returning one day, Marco finally got Kublai to agree to let him go. But on the way, Marco had to escort a royal princess to Persia via an eighteen-month sea voyage. Ships in the 1200s were filthy death traps full of rats, but this one was Marco's ride out of town. Because of disease, pirates, and every other awful shipboard thing, of the six hundred people who set sail, only eighteen made it to the final destination—including the princess and all three Polos.

After twenty-four years of servitude to either Khan or his father, in Asia, India, and Africa, Marco was finally free.

Marco arrived in Venice dressed in Mongol style. His hairdo was a combo of shaved areas, short tufts, and long braids, and he wore brightly colored silk pants and a coat-like robe called a "caftan."

He dressed differently, but Marco now looked forward to the quiet life of a merchant of Venice, sharing his past adventures without the threat of death. But people didn't believe that his outrageous stories were really true. How could they be? And Marco couldn't prove any of it.

After a few years as a salesman, with no purpose bigger than reconciling account books, Marco missed his old life. Being a wealthy merchant didn't compare to the wealth of his past experiences: Marco was a wanderer at heart.

Desperate to get moving, he jumped at the chance to *be somebody* again. He joined the Venice navy to fight Genoa, a nearby city-state, for control of the trade routes to the east. But at forty-four years old, Marco was practically the oldest in the navy. And he forgot he wasn't a warrior. Even in Marco's youth, Khan had seen that. After decades of getting along with all varieties of people from Acre to Zanzibar, Marco signed up to fight his neighbors in Genoa. What was he thinking?

Marco commanded one of the ninety-six galleys in the Venetian fleet. He hoped he'd find his mojo again.

But he didn't.

After a nine-hour battle, eighty-four of the galleys were either sunk, burned, or captured.

Lucky to be alive, Marco was thrown in jail as a prisoner of war.

Marco's cell mate in Genoa's prison was Rustichello of Pisa. He had been captured in a battle fourteen years earlier. Most prisoners start talking about their innocence, but Marco gave his bunk mate an earful of the Far East. Rustichello was a romance writer, and he knew a good story when he heard one. With nothing else to do, they collaborated:

Marco told his travel stories and Rustichello wrote them down—something Marco had never bothered to do.

And from that single handwritten copy of *Description of the World*—penned in prison—Marco Polo's legacy lives on. It was reproduced by hand for 179 years, one copy at a time, until the invention of the printing press changed the way books were made.

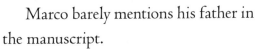

Marco barely mentions his father in the manuscript.

You'll hear Marco Polo's name while playing hide-and-seek on land and in a swimming pool, and there's absolutely no escaping his name in history books about the Silk Road, maps, Kublai Khan, and the Age of Discovery. Marco Polo lived a larger-than-life adventure, going around the world when everyone still thought it was flat.

Marco Polo was released from prison in 1299. Back in Venice, he married Donata Badoer, and they had three daughters. Marco died in 1324 at the age of seventy.

If Marco Polo hadn't been a total failure as a soldier, and if he hadn't been tossed in jail with Rustichello, we never would have known he even existed. And when there were no more roads for this world traveler, he (and his cell mate) created a permanent mind trip for the rest of us. Sometimes we think of a failure as the end, but it's not; it can be the road to success—as long as you don't choke—or irritate your jailer.

WHERE'D YOU GO, MARCO POLO?

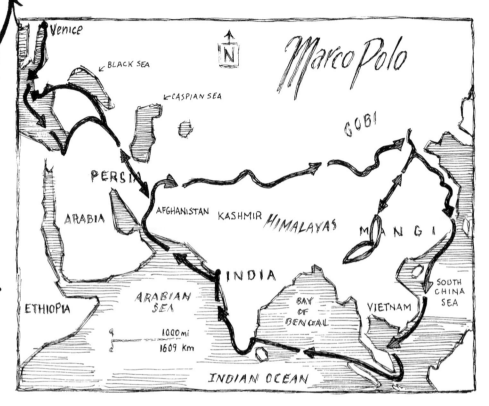

WHAT'S THE BIG DEAL ABOUT SILK?

SILK IS MADE FROM WORMS that originated in China. Silkworms spin cocoons of slender strands about half a mile long that are processed and woven into fabric. At one time, silk was as valuable as gold, and only royalty was allowed to wear it. If people tried to smuggle silkworms out of China or reveal the secret of how they were cultivated, they were put to death. But selling silk itself was very big business, since it was one of the main items Europeans wanted. As silk merchants traveled from East to West, their route became known as the *Silk* Road.

SELF-PUBLISHING SUCCESS STORY

Description of the World Known as His *Travels*
BY MARCO POLO

- Original handwritten manuscript, prison, Genoa, 1298
- Word of mouth spread that it was worth reading
- Nobles wanted a copy in their libraries
- Copyists handwrote it, translating it into many languages
- No two versions of the manuscript are alike
- Friar Francesco Pipino translated it into Latin, between 1310 and 1314
- Pipino added words like "hated" in every reference to Muslims or infidels, to prepare monks for establishing future religious missions in the East
- The first machine-printed version was in German, taken from Pipino's altered Latin text, 1477
- Marco Polo's original prison manuscript has disappeared

First Sentence of
Travels by Marco Polo

"Lords, Emperors, Kings, Dukes and Marquesses, Counts, Knights, and Burgesses, and all people who are pleased and wish to know the different generations of men and the diversities of the different regions and lands of the world, take then this book and have it read, and here you will find all the greatest marvels and the great diversities of the Greater and Lesser Armenia, and of Persia, Media, Turkey, and of the Tartars and India and of many other provinces about Asia Media and part of Europe, going toward the Greek wind, levant, and tramontaine, just as our book will tell you clearly in order, as Master Marco Polo, wise and noble citizen of Venice, relates because he saw them with his own eyes."

OMG

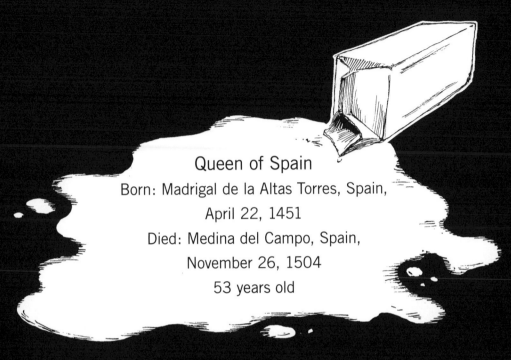

Queen of Spain
Born: Madrigal de la Altas Torres, Spain,
April 22, 1451
Died: Medina del Campo, Spain,
November 26, 1504
53 years old

THERE'S GOOD NEWS and bad news about Queen Isabella. She's admirable because she ran Spain when everybody told her a woman couldn't do it. And while she was running it she gave Christopher Columbus money to go exploring. She also believed in prayer. The bad news is she overdid everything. Isabella was the original get-out-of-my-way-and-don't-tell-me-what-to-do person. Those who didn't believe or want the same things she did had their limbs ripped apart, brains crushed, or body fried in a slow-burning fire. Queen Isabella's reign of terror was called the Spanish Inquisition.

No one paid much attention when Princess Isabella was born in 1451. Although she was the daughter of the king of Castile and León (occupying three-quarters of modern-day Spain), there was no hoopla when she was born because she was "just a girl." Unlike her two

brothers, who as boys got their own little kingdoms to practice ruling, with real people to boss around, all Isabella got was to call her brothers significant titles like "constable" and "his mastership" while learning to sew and aimlessly staring out a window. From day one, her parents were looking to match her up and send her off with a strange royal man from some faraway country to keep it from fighting them. That was her future.

When Isabella's older half brother Enrique IV became king of Castile, Isabella left court and was raised by her depressed, batty, churchgoing mother. At daily mass, Isabella was reminded by the teachings of the church that good girls were subservient to men. Maybe other girls bought that baloney, but not Isabella. She was smart, athletic, and able to do a lot more than just sew; Isabella rode horses and went bear hunting.

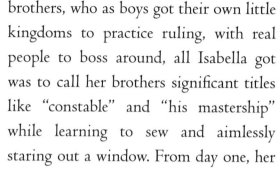

BEAR!

At eleven years old, Isabella was promised in marriage to the thirty-two-year-old king of Portugal, Afonso V. The first time Isabella met him, she was already smart enough to demand something from him he'd never be able to deliver: written approval of their marriage from all the nobles in her kingdom. The nobles never agreed about anything, so that worked. But her next prearranged engagement was with the groom-of-last-resort, the forty-three-year-old Don Pedro Girón, Master of Calatrava, a powerful and conniving old creep. Her king/brother wanted his loyalty, and giving him Isabella was a way to get it.

With no say in the matter, and no clear idea of how to squirm out of this one, Isabella just stopped eating, bawled her eyes out, and prayed endlessly it wouldn't happen. And big surprise, it worked. Girón dropped dead on his way to meet her. Her prayers had been answered. Isabella thought, "Wow!" She'd made someone drop dead just like that. Think of all the other stuff she could make happen. Her head started spinning with options.

Isabella spent a lot more time on her knees after that.

In her prayers, she was scheming to win control of the Castilian crown from her other brother, her niece, and numerous distant relations who also felt entitled to it. But Isabella believed the crown would be hers because God loved her the most. The royal infighting incited a civil war and helped trash the country that they all wanted to rule so much.

At eighteen, Isabella jumped at the chance to marry the charming seventeen-year-old prince Ferdinand of the way smaller neighboring territory of Aragon (one-quarter of modern-day Spain), even though her king/brother didn't approve. Ferdinand was born in the same decade as her, and even better, he wasn't old enough to be her father. She begged God for it to happen and it did. They met on a Saturday and were married by Wednesday. No one knew it at the time, but

Isabella and Ferdinand's two joined kingdoms would one day become Spain. The newlyweds had things in common too: they both went to Mass every day, and were list makers. Isabella had a list of people who owed her something.

On the list was Ferdinand's father, the king of Aragon. Isabella demanded he hand over the money that was due to her as part of the wedding package, ASAP. And she wanted him to honor his promise to give her some townships. Besides just badgering her father-in-law to send the money, she prayed to God that he would—until he did.

At twenty-three, Isabella became the queen of Castile after the death of her brother/king. Her other brother had either eaten poisoned fish or died of the plague. Whatever; he was dead, and her niece had a slight heir-apparent problem because the king might not have really been her dad. Isabella was next in line, and she would show everyone what a woman could accomplish. No one would ever tell Isabella what to do again.

Not even Ferdinand. She was crowned queen while Ferdinand was settling some skirmish in Aragon. He found out about it after the fact, but not from Isabella. She wrote him a letter but didn't even mention it. She knew he'd be mad. He was her coruler, but not really—she was the boss.

Ferdinand got a legal council together

Dear Ferdinand,
Everything is good at home.
Nothing has changed since you left.
I haven't made myself all-time BOSS. xo
ISABELLA

to try to force Isabella to give him more power. But Isabella was unmovable. Budging only slightly, Isabella allowed him to have his name listed first on all documents. She let Ferdinand punish criminals and wage war. But Isabella decided whether to finance his wars because she controlled the money, and chose the military and religious leaders. If they disagreed about anything, Isabella had the final say. Their publicity motto was, "One is equal to the other." Lip service was all Ferdinand got.

Castile was hers.

She believed it was her responsibility to whip her troubled country back into shape after years of war. The people lived in constant fear of crime, violence, and the runaway rat population. Her brother, the king before her, had granted favors and land to all the wrong people just so he could keep the crown, and no one wanted to give anything back. Each local domain had its own leaders with distinct religions and culture. Hostilities were ongoing between the clashing communities whether they were Jewish, Muslim, or Christian.

Isabella had a plan to make everyone get along and to rid her country of all its problems—and she would "do so with the help of God to make everything secure."

Running the country wasn't a spectator sport for Isabella. Unlike most queens, who'd order other people to make mistakes on their behalf, Isabella made her mistakes face-to-face. It didn't matter if she was almost nine months pregnant with one of her five children while on the road; with steely resolve she'd hop on a horse and ride into unruly towns and force everyone to do what she said. Now, everyone just feared her.

She hated disorder of any kind, and to fix it, Isabella decided to just blame the Jews and the Muslims for everything. She called it the "act of faith."

For the Jews of Castile, life had been hard for centuries already. They couldn't own land and weren't allowed to join trade unions or hold office. Many Jews converted to Christianity to survive. Muslims had done the same thing. Jews who hadn't converted had to wear a yellow badge and live in a separate neighborhood. But Isabella believed that the Jews who had converted still practiced Judaism in secret. The idea of pretend Christians bothered her so much she decided to do something about it. Isabella made it possible for people to snitch on whoever they thought might be heretics—those who didn't really believe the teachings of the Catholic Church. Or the heretics could turn themselves in. Otherwise, Isabella would find them and just kill them.

This became known as the Spanish Inquisition. The pope in Rome gave Isabella and Ferdinand's plan his blessing.

Isabella's inquisitors traveled from town to town and got right down to business; investigations started with torture. There was flogging, the ropes, the rack, and the pulley: contraptions that would yank joints apart, cut through muscles, and cause paralysis. Others caused blindness or ripped off body parts or drowned people, and had names like Iron Maiden and Spanish Spider. Heretics could also be burned alive in the town square. It was amazing how fast people confessed to avoid being tortured.

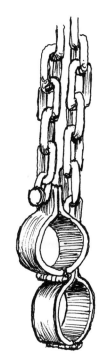

For the first time, an Inquisition was run by a monarchy, and not by the Church. Isabella paid for it, hired the staff, and oversaw the whole thing herself. She felt justified confiscating the property of the accused. Those sinners owed it to her.

In 1482, four years into it, the pope told Isabella to stop being so cruel and to show some compassion. He sent a memo: "The Inquisition has for some time been moved not by zeal for the faith and the salvation of souls, but by lust and wealth. . . ." The pope no longer condoned Isabella's Inquisition.

Isabella refused to obey the pope's list of reforms. She thought she was a better Catholic than the pope. And she had news for the pope too: it's not just a man's world anymore, and I'm proving that. She was the law because she said she was, and nobody—not even His Holiness—could mess with Isabella. Besides, what was the big deal? Torturing and burning heretics who deviated from the holy Catholic faith was a small price to pay to keep her God happy. It was her duty to do it. Ferdinand was behind her all the way.

Delusional and out of control, Isabella terrified everyone.

What kind of queen would want to be so merciless and make her people suffer?

After torturing, killing, and imprisoning thousands, Isabella decided to just get rid of the rest of the Jews with her Edict of Expulsion. But first, they were to leave all their gold and money with her. She "decreed to order all Jews of both sexes to leave the confines of our lands forever." Signed, "I, the Queen." Of course that didn't include her financial adviser or her doctor, who both happened to be Jews who had converted to Christianity. They were ordered to stay, along with all the gold and money belonging to her former Jewish subjects.

After she had taken care of the Jews, and run the Muslims out of the neighboring kingdom of Granada and taken it over, the combined kingdoms formed the beginning of what we now know as Spain.

In 1492, the Inquisition in Spain was at its zenith when she gave money (paid for by "secret Jews") to Christopher Columbus to push off into unknown waters. Ferdinand was less enthused. Greed and the hunt for more people to convert were Isabella's motivations in supporting Columbus; he was to find gold and give it to her, and to name anything he found after guess who.

During the first two decades of the Spanish Inquisition, while Isabella and Ferdinand were running it, about two thousand people were put to death. That's approximately one ritual killing every few days. Their children continued the Inquisition after they died.

Isabella created a society that systematically told some of its people they were no good. There had been other Inquisitions, but nobody did it quite like Isabella. The Spanish Inquisition started in 1478, spread through Europe, and lasted for three hundred and fifty years, well into the 1800s. About three hundred thousand people eventually stood trial, with 1.5 million witnesses and informers— and that was just in Isabella's neck of the woods. About twelve thousand people lost their lives in the Spanish Inquisition.

The Spanish traveled immense distances around the globe. Christopher Columbus was free to explore, but he took Isabella's point of view—that everyone should be a Catholic—across the ocean with him. The quest for gold and riches spared no one.

Queen Isabella's story is too good and too bad not to tell. It's a historical and a cautionary tale. Driven by her perverse duty to God, Isabella was a dangerous fanatic. With an obsessive zeal for one thing only, there is no balance in life. You miss every other possibility open to you. If Isabella had really understood the teachings of the Church she would have realized they included kindness, charity, understanding, and forgiveness. Instead, Isabella of Spain was bigoted, close-minded, and cruel, the exact opposite of what a good queen should be.

ISABELLA AND FERDINAND'S CHILDREN

1. Isabella of Castile and Aragon   1470–1498
2. Juan of Castile and Aragon   1478–1497
3. Joanna of Castile   1479–1555
   Known as Joanna the Mad,
   suffered from mental illness
4. María of Aragon   1482–1517
5. **Katherine of Aragon**   1485–1536

KATHERINE OF ARAGON MARRIED HENRY VIII OF ENGLAND, and their daughter was Mary Tudor, better known as "Bloody Mary." She was into prosecuting English Protestants in the same way Grandma Isabella prosecuted Jews and Muslims in Spain. Mary burned 274 people at the stake, including the archbishop of Canterbury.

MAP OF THE IBERIAN PENINSULA AND THE KINGDOMS OF SPAIN IN THE 1500S

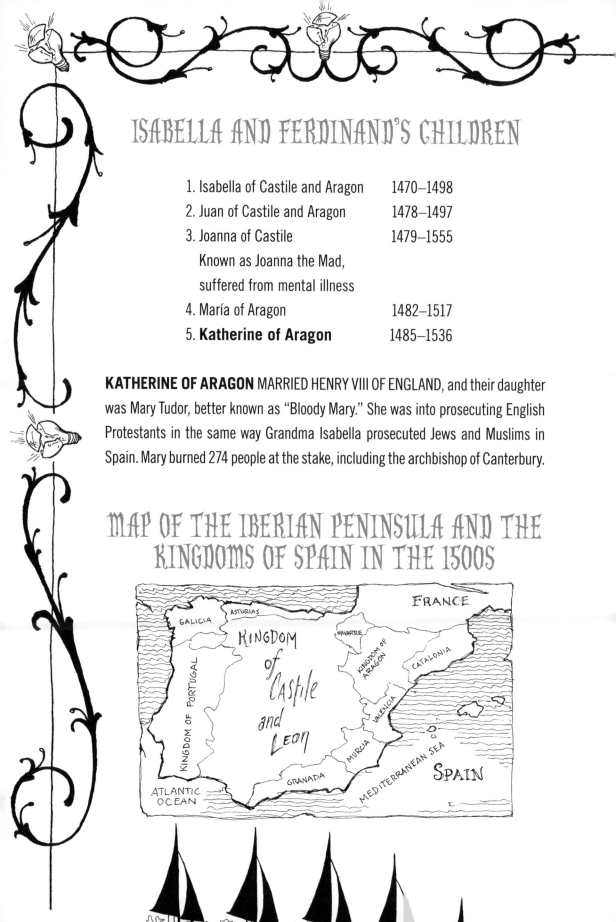

GRAND INQUISITOR OF SPAIN

Tomás de Torquemada
1420–1498

ISABELLA APPOINTED TOMÁS DE TORQUEMADA as Grand Inquisitor of the Spanish Inquisition. Torquemada spent fifteen fanatical years hunting down heretics (people who didn't believe in the same things as the Catholic Church) in Spain. He probably gave Isabella the idea to run all the Jews out of Spain. Torquemada wrote an instruction manual for inquisitors with tips on torture and confinement. Girls as young as twelve and boys of fourteen could be called into the Inquisition for questioning. Years after Torquemada died, his bones were stolen and then burned.

BURNED ALIVE AT THE STAKE

Burning at the stake was the preferred punishment during
Isabella's Spanish Inquisition

First used: February 6, 1481

Where: Campo de Tablada, Seville, Spain

Who: six men and women burned on the first day

Why: Jews accused of "Judaizing" (returning to their former religion) and conspiring against the crown

Convicted by: Alonso de Hojeda, a Dominican friar and a founding member of the Inquisition in Spain

Grisly death by: smoke inhalation, intense heat, seared trachea, edema, damaged nerves and tissues, asphyxiation, hypovolemic shock, or pulmonary failure

Spain's last Inquisition execution: 1826, Cayetano Ripoll, convicted of heresy and hanged, not burned at the stake

MONTEZUMA II

OOPS, THERE GO THE AZTECS

Emperor of the Aztecs
Born: Tenochtitlán, Mexico,
1466
Died: Tenochtitlán, Mexico,
June 30, 1520
54 years old

PERHAPS MONTEZUMA II'S problem was that he took all things Aztec way over the top. It's unimaginable today, but the Aztecs feared that if they didn't sacrifice people through brutal deaths it would never rain again and the crops wouldn't grow. Montezuma II, Emperor of the Aztecs, was known for his superstitions and his delight in ripping out people's ticking hearts, literally, on a regular basis. It was that kind of bloody stuff that made the Aztec culture what it was. Sure, the Aztecs had chocolate, maize on the cob, and pyramids, and their scary masks fill our museums, but the whole killing-obsessed Aztec Empire and its ruler were stuck in a time warp. And when Montezuma was threatened by an outsider, the lines between good and evil, real and unreal, became so twisted and blurred, he didn't know how to save himself or his people.

In 1466, Montezuma II was born into a long line of chiefs, kings, and emperors in the city of Tenochtitlán, which today is Mexico City. The Aztec people followed a bunch of not-so-healthy customs that involved drowning children and then calling them lunch. It wasn't for lack of food, but lack of enlightenment. But baby Montezuma was ordained to stay intact; the ruling party didn't eat their own. The monarchy was a single-family business, and titles were passed around to uncles and nephews and other close relations. The family would hang around sharing the same anecdotes about how perfect everything was and how they should never change anything. Boys were sent to boarding schools, called "houses of tears." And we can guess Montezuma never had the option to say, "I don't want to go to school today." The goal was to squash students' curiosity about everything except going to war. By the age of eighteen, the young men were combat ready and expected to go off to some battle or other and bring home a prisoner of war, and then torture the captive in front of a live Aztec audience. For Montezuma, proving himself as a warrior in this way was just the first step for advancement within the family monarchy business.

As he moved up the ranks, Montezuma showed his commitment to upholding the family name, along with enforcing the law. Not a lot of contemplation was involved for Montezuma because in his culture there was no forgiveness, understanding, or rehabilitation—every crime was punishable by death. Just wearing cotton clothes could do it, or if you fouled or erred in their athletic ball game, which was a blend of basketball and soccer, you would be decapitated. Absolutely no one was having any fun, and eventually Montezuma was in charge of seeing to it.

Scary sports aside, the main purpose in life for an Aztec man, besides being a warrior, was to serve the gods. Which soaked up a lot of the day because there were hundreds of them. Every Aztec home had an altar. The honored "big four" were the gods of the sun, rain, fire, and maize. Professions and objects had gods too, like the feathered-headdress-maker god, the wood-chiseler god, and the hoe-and-shovel god. Ritualized murders were necessary to keep these gods happy. So a person had to be sacrificed in the sun god's honor to make the sun come back up after it had disappeared the night before, and the victims were brainwashed into thinking this was a great way to go.

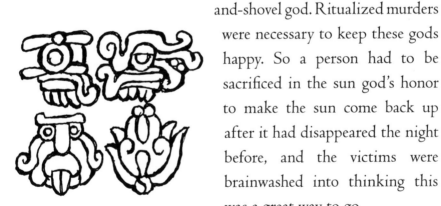

As a young noble, Montezuma was crazy-devoted to the gods, and this was noticed by the present emperor (who happened to be Montezuma's uncle), leading him to choose Montezuma to be one of only two high priests. His main job requirement was to figure out whose blood pleased which god, and especially to focus on Huitzilopochtli, the god of war and sacrifice, and Tlaloc, the really needy god of rain. Following tradition, Montezuma dyed his body black and sliced off hunks of his own ears so he could dribble his blood all over the temple as an offering. Seasonal ritual killings were important—and frightening, because for many, if it was summer, they'd be spending it as a corpse. His duties to the deities included temple watchman, staring at the sky, and blowing into a conch shell to start battles. But most of the time he anointed the temple pyramids with blood from the thousands of victims who were held down while their still-beating hearts were removed and their heartless bodies tossed down the hundred and fourteen steps to the ground. Only a lunatic would want this job.

But then Montezuma got a big job promotion. His family picked him as the new emperor. At thirty-seven years old, he was ready for his real career. The emperorship would be his, but first he had to attack a rebel region and bring back a throng of captives so that their blood could be splattered around for good luck at his coronation. Montezuma proceeded with gusto. After many festivals in his honor, Emperor Montezuma led his armies to overtake opposing cities, expanding the empire's land, power, and wealth, and making sure there would be enough captives to bring back and sacrifice to the gods. Montezuma was the warlord of about a million people in cities stretching from the Gulf of Mexico to the Pacific Ocean, and all the way to what is now Guatemala.

Montezuma let his army fight without him so he could stay home and make sure the royal palace was worthy of him. He spent his days picking out feathered drapery, enlarging the aviary, decorating the fountains and pools, and adding new animals to his zoo. Everyone thought he was doing a great job remodeling the place as ostentatiously as possible, but his head was getting way too big for the doorway, and he was obsessed with himself. As a matter of fact, Montezuma considered himself a semi-god, which meant he got carried around everywhere, and anyone who looked right at him or talked right to him would be killed. Those even allowed in his presence had to wear a plain sack over their nice clothes so that the emperor looked especially great and they didn't. And since he changed his clothes four times a day and never wore the same thing twice, he wanted to make sure everyone noticed.

After seventeen years of this, forget being a semi-god, the coldhearted leader acted like a real living god. And everyone let him do it because they were too brainwashed and afraid of him to say, "Hey, you're just a man."

But Montezuma's days were numbered. The future was passing his isolated civilization by, mostly because he believed what lay ahead was already set in stone.

Around the world, Leonardo da Vinci had painted the *Mona Lisa*, Michelangelo had sculpted *David*, and the first mechanically printed

Bible had been produced. Columbus had sailed to the New World, claiming it for Spain. Another Spanish explorer, Hernán Cortés, had followed in Columbus's wake to claim more lands for Spain.

In 1519, Hernán Cortés landed on the shores of Mexico with an army of five hundred men, sixteen horses, and lots of weapons. And just like Montezuma, Cortés was into empire expansion (for Spain, though) right in Mexico—Montezuma's backyard.

On his arrival, Cortés blasted off his weaponry and galloped the horses down the beach. No one had ever seen such an animal in the New World before. Cortés assured the horrified people that he only wanted food even though his real plan was to take everything and kill them all.

Montezuma heard about Cortés's ability to make fire and thunder on command, and how his white skin and beard were exactly like

those of the legendary Quetzalcóatl, the god of air. There were statues of Quetzalcóatl all over the place, and everyone worshipped him. When Quetzalcóatl lived on Earth there was peace, plants thrived, and the air around him smelled of perfume. He believed that only fruits and flowers should be sacrificed, not people. Quetzalcóatl had sailed away, but was due to sail back and rule again—and according to the Aztec calendar it was the exact year he was supposed to return.

The idea of another living god in the vicinity was bad news for Montezuma. Not to mention he'd have to give up his newly renovated palace. He sent Cortés feathered clothing, gold jewelry, and precious stones to show his wealth and power along with a stern message for Cortés to get lost. But all those golden treasures Montezuma sent made Cortés march inland even faster.

Montezuma's nobles advised him to kill the Spanish invaders; they were trespassing and disrespecting him. Undecided, Montezuma slipped inside the temple and stayed for days and days, searching for a sign. Montezuma didn't want to make a mistake and kill the second coming of Quetzalcóatl. The cosmic consequences for him would be colossal. After deep contemplation, he decided to send his best magicians to put Cortés under a spell. After that failed, his advisers were furious and confused; killing was their go-to option for everything. They waited for Montezuma to give the word, but he stalled and stalled.

Nine months later Cortés arrived in the heart of the Aztec Empire, and came face-to-face with Montezuma.

Montezuma leaned in to see if Cortés smelled like perfume. Satisfied, Montezuma welcomed the returning god and gave him the keys to the palace while everyone looked on in shock. And thinking Cortés/Quetzalcóatl the returning god would be pleased, Montezuma took him inside the private inner chamber of the temple to visit the bloodstained war-god statue, the big burning basin for human hearts, and the blood-covered priests performing the gods' work. Cortés thanked him by launching into a lecture, telling Montezuma to quit it with the sacrifices to all those gods; it was creepy. Even more shocking, Cortés believed there was only one god, and he put up a cross in the temple to honor him.

Montezuma now realized he had been wrong about Cortés. He was no god, and Montezuma should have killed him like everyone kept telling him to do. But it was too late. Cortés imprisoned Montezuma inside his own palace. Cornered, Montezuma didn't know what to do next, so he did nothing.

With their emperor imprisoned, the Aztec warriors attacked the invaders. A full-blown war raged on for weeks between the few hundred Spaniards and tens of thousands of Aztecs. Even though the Aztecs outnumbered the enemy, their out-of-date sticks and rocks were no match for cannons and guns. But their weapons weren't

Spanish Rifle

Aztec Spear

totally useless, after all, because when Montezuma appeared, shackled in irons, and pleaded with his people to stop fighting, the stones and spears hurled right at him killed him on the spot. Montezuma died on June 30, 1520, killed by his own people.

Montezuma's violent seventeen-year regime was over. He was not missed after he died. Maybe his people hoped the violence would finally stop, but they were wrong. Cortés put an end to all things Aztec, including all the people. After only a few years, they had been wiped out by war and disease.

Montezuma had allowed his superstitions and ego to cloud his reasoning. Unable to face change or new ideas, Montezuma's closed mind doomed him to fail. He was at the helm of a culture gone mad, and he was unwilling to alter it. Inaction is a powerful decision. Montezuma turned himself into a museum piece, and he took the entire Aztec culture with him.

MONTEZUMA'S REVENGE

WHEN TOURISTS VISIT MEXICO AND drink from the local water supply or eat food with unfamiliar bacteria, it can cause diarrhea or what some call "the runs." Tourists' diarrhea is called "Montezuma's Revenge," because supposedly this is how Montezuma is getting even with foreigners entering Mexico. It's also been called the "Aztec Two-Step."

AZTEC GODS AND GODDESSES

Huitzilopochtli: god of war and sacrifice

Xiuhtecuhtli: god of fire

Tonatiuh: sun god

Tlaloc: rain god

Centéotl: god of maize

Xipe Totec: god of agriculture

Ehecatl: god of wind

Ixtlilton: god of medicine and healing

PYRAMID DESIGN

THE STEPS ON AZTEC PYRAMIDS are very steep. After a human sacrifice was completed at the top, the body was thrown off, and the only way to ensure that the corpse tumbled all the way down to the bottom without stopping was to design extra-steep steps.

EIGHT AZTEC EMPERORS AND THEIR RELATIONSHIP TO MONTEZUMA II

TITLE	NAME	REIGN	RELATIONSHIP
First Emperor	Itzcoatl	1428–1440	Great-grandfather
Second Emperor	Montezuma I	1440–1469	Great-uncle
Third Emperor	Axayacatl	1469–1481	Father
Fourth Emperor	Tizoc	1481–1486	Uncle
Fifth Emperor	Ahuitzotl	1486–1502	Uncle
Sixth Emperor	**Montezuma II**	1502–1520	Himself

Two more relatives struggled to stay in power, but they didn't last long.

Seventh Emperor	Cuitlahuac	1520	Brother
Eighth Emperor	Cuauhtemoc	1520–1521	Cousin

TABLE FOR ONE

MONTEZUMA WOULDN'T LET ANYONE WATCH him eat so he ate alone. For each meal, hundreds of prepared dishes were spread out on the floor. After he had chosen his favorites, a gold-embellished wooden screen was drawn around him. Inside his little makeshift enclosure, Montezuma sat on a floor cushion and chowed down at a small, low table for one. His empty plates were never allowed to be reused.

Montezuma drank no beverage other than *chocolatl*, an Aztec chocolate drink. It had the consistency of honey, and he ate it with a spoon.

FERDINAND MAGELLAN

DEAD IN THE WATER

Explorer
Born: Sabrosa, Portugal,
circa 1480
Died: Mactan Island, Philippines,
April 27, 1521
41 years old

FERDINAND MAGELLAN WAS a cold, strict man who felt entitled to everything. These traits worked well, given that he was a major player in the Age of Discovery. That was when Europeans went here and there around the world and took over places where people already lived, renamed them, and called them discoveries. Magellan has the reputation of being the first man to sail around the world— and that story's not going anywhere—because he only made it a little more than halfway. Magellan's tactics of terror cut his trip short. Any sailing trip was risky business in the 1500s, but seafaring dangers were the least of everyone's concerns; there was Magellan to worry about.

Even though Magellan's parents didn't write down the date he was born, they did know that they had a slight genetic connection to the royal family of Portugal, and they milked it. So when Magellan was twelve-ish, he was shipped off to Lisbon to get educated in the royal court. One of his duties was to prepare ships for voyages. After Magellan had soaked up sailor talk such as "monkey-rigged," "poop," and "parley" for ten years, King Manuel of Portugal assigned him to board a ship bound for India. Even in the cramped quarters of ships, there is no mention of Magellan making any friends, only that he was sturdy, dark, and not tall.

Magellan fought in a lot of battles for the king of Portugal, capturing towns and establishing trading posts. He was a great fighter, sailor, and navigator, but not so great a communicator, especially when demanding the king buy him a new horse or give him a bigger paycheck. King Manuel thought Magellan was a royal pain, but somehow he moved up in the ranks of ship life.

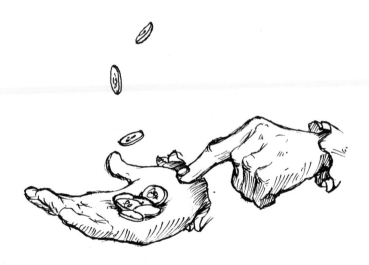

Magellan studied charts and secret maps with sea routes to fabulous places where fortunes could be made on spices—hopefully without paying a dime. Back then, people wanted cloves and other spices for cooking (just as much as people today want oil to make fuel), and they would do anything to get them. Magellan was sure the shortest distance between the spices and his ship was a straight line, and he knew where that line was—right through South America, avoiding the treacherous waters of Cape Horn. Four times he begged the king to bankroll a voyage to the place Europeans had named the Spice Islands, although of course it already had its own name, the Moluccas. But the king loathed Magellan, so the answer was always no.

Then, to make the situation worse, Magellan took his slightly regal self and moved to Spain. At the time, Spain and Portugal thought they had dibs on everything in the world. The two kingdoms made an imaginary dividing line through the itty-bitty world they had on their maps, which showed only three continents and two oceans. That's four continents and three oceans short of the real deal, including the Pacific Ocean, which covers a third of the planet. A signed treaty officially set the rule for the two countries: stay on your own side of the line or die.

So King Manuel considered Magellan a traitor for changing sides. Magellan's relatives back in Portugal were stoned, and their homes were looted.

In Spain, Magellan's new country, King Charles I welcomed the navigator with his top-secret info about Portuguese sailing maps, even though he knew Magellan wasn't to be fully trusted.

But Magellan didn't really care whose side he sailed on; he just needed someone to pay for it.

Magellan married Beatriz Barbosa, his slightly royal soul mate, and thanks to her connections, he soon had access to King Charles of Spain. This time, Magellan pitched the idea that the Spice Islands

were on Spain's side on the map of the world—and he knew a way to get there. King Charles was all for it; he made Magellan captain general of five ships and told Magellan to go find himself a crew.

Local Spanish sailors didn't want to sail with a Portuguese captain, so Magellan cobbled together the most international crew that ever sailed. They couldn't understand each other about most things, but luckily they knew the international nautical Castilian language, with a name for every hook, line, and sinker on board so they wouldn't capsize.

Most sailors were in their teens and twenties. Avoiding debtor's prison or hanging were good reasons to hop on board. Boys as young as eight came too. Men in their thirties were considered old, so at almost forty, Magellan was the ancient mariner. The crew of 257 was made up of kids, murderers, card sharks, crooks, and career sailors. The king filled the remaining ranks

with Spanish officers who'd keep an eye on Magellan's every move. As if the whole adventure wasn't dangerous enough, most of the crew couldn't swim.

Four-fifths of what they packed to eat out in the middle of nowhere was wine and hockey puck–like biscuits called hardtack. And no one left shore without a rod and fish bait. Magellan took a personal stash of thirty-five boxes of preserved quince (think apple jam).

They also brought ten cannons, three tons of gunpowder, fifty shotguns, one thousand spears, one hundred suits of armor, sixty crossbows, and four thousand arrows. As well as a bunch of leg irons and manacles to put on the people they wouldn't outright kill.

To deal with the locals they couldn't scare to death, they packed junk to trade. There were twenty thousand bells, five hundred pounds of beads and bracelets, almost five thousand dull knives, and a thousand little hand mirrors. With everything loaded aboard, they were good to go, setting sail on September 20, 1519.

Then Magellan caught wind that King Manuel of Portugal had sent a bunch of ships to intercept his fleet and arrest him as a traitor. To dodge the Portuguese ships, Magellan sailed on an unplanned crazy route that didn't make sense to anyone. When probed, Magellan just told his crew, "Ask no questions," never once mentioning that he was just saving his own fore-and-aft. He sailed them straight into life-threatening storms for sixty days, then into dead calm for three weeks, while drastically reducing their rations. And they hadn't even gotten anywhere yet.

The crew's desperation made no difference to Magellan. Three agonizing months later, they disembarked in Rio de Janeiro, Brazil. The sailors partied hard and had fun, probably a lot more fun than the Brazilians they were with. After replenishing their supplies they pushed off.

Hugging the coast of South America, they sailed south down the Atlantic Ocean looking for a strait. Magellan was still denying the crew full rations. The crew thought Magellan was on a suicide mission and that the strait he kept talking about didn't even exist. And if they didn't turn back soon, they'd freeze to death.

They stopped in Port Saint Julian, Patagonia, for five and a half frozen months to wait out the Antarctic winter. There was no edible vegetation and the water was lousy. The few locals were friendly, but the merciless Magellan tricked them aboard his ship and then shackled them in irons. Next Magellan went after his own crew. He

had one sailor strangled on the beach because he didn't follow orders. Others were hanged, drawn, and quartered, and two men were abandoned in the middle of nowhere.

Magellan sent one ship ahead down the coastline to hunt for the strait. The thirty-seven men were so glad to be away from Magellan, they docked at a bay and had a luau. When they finally set sail to do what Magellan had ordered them to do, a huge storm sank their ship. The men survived, but in the freezing weather they had to hike seventy miles back to the fleet.

That seemed like another great reason to ditch the search for the strait, but instead, it just confirmed the crew's worst fear: the captain general was going to risk their lives on his crusade no matter what.

After two more grueling months, on October 21, 1520, they finally found the strait—and it was a maze. The crew thought they should go back to Spain and get better equipped. They were weak and hungry. Magellan assessed the narrow waterways, glaciers, gale-force winds, and dangerous ice formations hanging out over the water, and still decided to sail onward. Now they faced 334 miles of strait jeopardy.

Again, Magellan sent one ship ahead to scout the unknown waters. Except the ship didn't sail forward; the crew turned around and sailed back home to Spain.

A ship defecting was bad enough, but it was also the ship that carried most of the remaining food.

It took thirty-eight days for the last three ships to sail from the Atlantic Ocean to the Pacific Ocean through the strait. Although Magellan was a madman, it was the single greatest accomplishment in the history of seafaring exploration.

But the men on board weren't that impressed.

Once through the strait, they were spilled out into the largest body of water in the world—the Pacific Ocean. It covers a greater area than all the land in the world combined, and is twice the size of the Atlantic Ocean. Magellan knew little about it; his maps were missing 80 percent of it, and a new set of stars were in the sky so he didn't know which direction to sail.

The Spice Islands should have been right there. But they weren't. Magellan wanted to know, who had taken his Spice Islands? As if

they didn't have enough to worry about with water stretching out to the horizon in every direction, they were down to eating sawdust, leather, and rats. The crew was dying of scurvy—all except Magellan, who was snacking on his private stash of quince preserves.

Ninety-eight days and seven thousand miles later, the survivors had swollen tongues. They pulled up to a crumb of land, the island of Guam. The innocently curious locals paddled out to meet the ships, hopped on board, and picked up everything they could get their hands on. The concept of ownership wasn't part of their culture. Magellan's thinking was, we take from *you*, not the other way around, so when someone took Magellan's personal dinghy to shore, the islanders got a taste of Magellan's lopsided justice. He set their village on fire, and killed seven of them. No one put up a fight when Magellan took his dinghy back.

Next they sailed to the seven thousand or so islands that made up the Philippines. It didn't exist on European maps, but there it was. They went island-hopping, and friendly locals greeted the weary travelers and gave them food. In return, Magellan fired his arsenal of weapons and cannons, which always horrified his new friends. He dressed a sailor in full metal armor and staged sword fights to show the islanders that he would win any fight—so don't even think about it. And whatever you do, don't take my dinghy.

Whenever Magellan found a safe harbor, he would drop anchor and the men would go ashore. The crew felt lucky they were on land because this year they could perform Easter mass on the beach. The locals watched the ceremonies. Magellan erected a large cross on the highest mountain and told the local island's king that the cross would stop lightning and storms from harming his people.

This was the start of a Magellan crusade: Magellan went around telling the people that if they became Christians, they'd receive extra-special treatment. Although they barely understood what he was talking about, he'd hand them a little bell or a mirror, and then they said, sure. Baptism not based on faith was directly against the Church's principles. But Magellan baptized eight hundred men, women, and children who had no idea what they were doing.

Then Magellan threatened to kill those who wouldn't convert. Just to show he wasn't kidding around, he set fire to fifty homes on a neighboring island whose chief hadn't converted yet. This tactic cemented the chief's resolve not to obey Magellan.

No more trinkets for that chief; Magellan would show him who was boss.

Magellan was way off course now. His crew begged him to stay focused on finding the Spice Islands, but Magellan wouldn't listen. He dressed in full armor and dragged sixty crew members to fight with him. It would be easy to fight off those islanders with their flimsy bamboo spears, right?

Fifteen hundred men from the village Magellan had just burned down, all with excellent spear skills, were ready to fight. Screaming at the top of their lungs, the islanders attacked, hitting Magellan in the thigh with a poison-tipped spear, and leaping on the other men. Once they realized which soldier was Magellan, they savagely killed him, hurling another spear into his face.

They hacked Magellan to bits. Even his own men didn't come to his aid.

The Age of Discovery was also the Age of Stupidity.

Only one ship and eighteen men made it back to Spain. Those eighteen men were the ones who actually sailed around the world. They had been gone for three years, crossed the equator four times, and traveled almost sixty thousand miles. They found the Spice Islands without Magellan, and they brought back 381 bags of cloves.

Besides being remembered for discovering the Strait of Magellan, which is named after him, Magellan is still known as the first explorer to circumnavigate the Earth. He died on April 27, 1521, and every year the Filipinos stage a reenactment of Magellan's death—that's how happy they were to see him die.

When you think you're always right, and everything is "mine, mine, mine"—and you're past the terrible twos—it's time to rethink your life.

The only peril Magellan couldn't survive was himself.

THE FIVE OCEANS

- The five oceans cover 71 percent of the earth's surface.
- Of all the water on earth, 97 percent is salt water.

ARCTIC: named for its proximity to the Arctic
ATLANTIC: named for its proximity to the Atlas Mountains
INDIAN: named for its proximity to India
PACIFIC: named Mar Pacifico or Peaceful Sea by Magellan in 1521
SOUTHERN: named for its proximity to southern places
GEOGRAPHY DRAMA!: The Southern Ocean did not officially become an ocean until 2000, but still not all geographers call it an ocean. Some believe it is simply an extension of the other four oceans.

NOT-SO-COOL FACT

About 3,700 shipwrecks from World War II lie at the bottom of the Pacific. All of them pose environmental hazards because of the oil, weapons, and chemicals on board when they sunk. It's not all gold doubloons down there. It's toxic waste and machine guns too!

425 YEARS LATER

IN 1521, MAGELLAN CLAIMED THE PHILIPPINES FOR SPAIN, paving the way for many battles to come between the Spanish, the natives, and everyone else who wanted the Philippines for themselves. In fact, thanks to Magellan, the Philippines would not gain back their independence until 1946—425 *years later*!

OTHER EXPLORERS KILLED BY THE NATIVE POPULATION

	EXPLORER	DEATH
1519	Alonso Alvarez de Pineda (Spanish)	Killed in what is now Texas
1521	Juan Ponce de León (Spanish)	Wounded by the Calusa Indians in Florida, made it to Cuba before dying
1528	Giovanni da Verrazzano (Italian)	Killed and eaten by Caribs tribe on the island of Guadeloupe
1539	Stephen the Moor (Spanish)	Killed in New Mexico by the Zuni
1779	James Cook (English)	Killed by locals in Hawaii

GRUB ON BOARD SHIP

wine • hardtack • anchovies • sardines
salt cod • salt beef • salt pork • olive oil
vinegar • beans • lentils • garlic
flour • rice • cheese • honey
sugar • raisins

Taken alive and killed during the journey:
7 cows • 3 pigs

ANNE BOLEYN

TILL BEHEADING DO US PART

Queen of England
Born: Norfolk, England,
circa 1501
Died: London, England,
May 19, 1536
35 years old

HENRY VIII WAS the only king in English history to have had six wives. It definitely made him *the* Henry, and he was quite a catch for a nobody like Anne Boleyn. But then again, Henry never met a lady-in-waiting he didn't like. Anne was wife number two, but even she should have seen the signs: Henry VIII was not marriage material. The guy banished his first wife, and pretended the twenty-odd years he had spent with her didn't count. He even disowned his own daughter. Anne Boleyn didn't want to see the fine print: in the vow "till death do us part" Henry picks when. But Anne Boleyn thought she could change the guy, and also predict the sex of her unborn child. Mostly, she was blinded by the crown jewels. But all the gold and titles in the world don't make up for a bad choice of life mate.

Rumor has it Anne Boleyn was born around 1501, but it's been confirmed that she was a middle child. She had an older sister and a younger brother so she needed to go the extra mile to get any attention. The Boleyns qualified for the lowest rung of the 1 percent of the population that had all the money and power.

Anne was smart, good on the lute, and graceful at dancing around in big dresses while trying desperately to get everyone to look at her and not at her big sister, Mary. Anne had an extra fingernail on one finger; some people claimed she had a whole extra finger. Either way, she liked covering it with a long sleeve. At about eleven years old Anne got a position in the court of Margaret of Austria, and then eventually moved on to the French court of Queen Claude and King Francis I as a lady-in-waiting, where she met up with her older sister, Mary. A lady-in-waiting was trained as a secretary, embroiderer, party girl extraordinaire, and living laugh track for all the queen's jokes.

52

During seven years of saying *"Je m'appelle* Anne," and eating snails and things smothered in mustard, she gradually became very French. While Anne conjugated verbs, her sister, Mary, learned how to French-kiss all the men, including King Francis I. Mary was just so darn popular and easy to be with, she eventually had to be thrown out after all  the men at court grew tired of her. Anne honed her skills, and grew up to be okay to look at if you didn't mind thin lips and enough cute moles to play connect the dots. They say her black eyes did all the talking, and she had the gift of gab that men liked, or you could just call her a flirt. Both Boleyn girls had that unteachable head-turning something that everybody secretly wished they had: "sex appeal."

At twenty, Anne was reassigned to Henry VIII's court in the employ of his wife, Queen Katherine of Aragon. Katherine was thirty-six, which back then qualified her as a senior citizen. Her baby-making talents were worn out from her six pregnancies, and she had only one living child, Princess Mary, to show for it. Since only men could run England up to that time, Katherine had failed to produce an heir to the throne. It was possible that Henry VIII would be the last of the Tudor clan to live in the royal castles.

Even though castles were cold, damp, stinky places, they were hard to give up. Dogs, birds, and even monkeys ran wild and relieved themselves (so did the men) in the layer of rushes that covered the floors. The only carpeted areas were the royal apartments. The people

were wild too; it was a generation of slandering, backstabbing, and head removal—and that was between friends. If you think it was romantic, it wasn't—men wore tights.

Henry VIII was thirty-one and he looked so-so in his royal Spanx. He enjoyed making up laws that worked in his favor, power-eating, and spending time with his wife's ladies-in-waiting. Henry's current darling was Anne's sister, Mary. Daddy Boleyn didn't mind Mary's behavior because Henry was promoting him left and right.

Anne was sick of being second best. She found herself her own Henry—Henry Percy. He wasn't the king, but he was in line for an earldom. They were secretly engaged, but the wedding never happened. Anne was a nobody, and nobodies weren't allowed to marry somebodies.

Anne was furious, and was sent away to cool down. Meanwhile, her sister got to stay at court and continue her affair with the king. It was so unfair!

About a year later Anne came back to the queen's household and by that time, Henry had tired of her sister, Mary. She had been sent away with no money and no chance of ever marrying into a respectable family. She was ruined.

Henry had decided his next lady-in-waiting-with-benefits would be Anne. Except she was adamantly *not* interested in a man who had already been with her sister. She had seen the consequences up close. There was too much at stake, and besides, the guy was already married.

Not accustomed to being a man-in-waiting for anything, Henry hounded Anne. She made herself scarce and got out of court as if her life depended on it. Anne's instincts were right, but sometimes he'd go out to find her, or he'd woo her with deer meat. Anne stayed aloof. His love letters arrived often. She barely responded.

Nothing would stop him from getting what he wanted. Henry VIII told Anne he would dump Queen Katherine for her, and then he handed Anne some diamonds, rubies, and some really pretty pajamas. Anne became less aloof. He was far from perfect, but she really liked his address. She went back to court to check out the new apartment Henry had prepared for her. It was a good offer for a girl like her, but she wanted more—actually she wanted it all—the pajamas, the deer meat, the jewels, but mostly she wanted to be the queen.

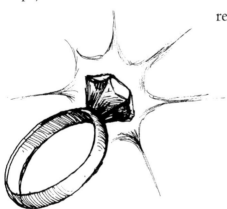

Queen Katherine figured Anne was just another woman Henry would eventually get tired of, like he always did. But not this time. Henry came up with a plan to prove that his marriage to Katherine was illegal because Katherine had originally been married to his older brother, Prince Arthur, until he died six months after the wedding. In the eyes of the church it was illegal to marry your brother's widow, but Katherine swore that her marriage to Henry's brother had never been consummated, and that she had stayed in the family by marrying Henry VIII. If the pope in Rome believed Henry and declared his first marriage null and void, he'd be a free man. Henry laid out the plan for Anne.

Maybe she had misjudged him after all. Then Anne made Henry a promise that he couldn't refuse—to give him a son. Make me queen, and you'll see, she said. There was a positive sign when her dad was promoted from viscount to Lord Privy Seal. She was really showing up her sister now, and she was going to change Henry into a better man.

They waited for the pope to decide. Besides being busy surviving the Sack of Rome, this pope had a bad case of indecision. He'd confirm a truce, undo a truce, make an alliance, end an alliance. At least he didn't change his mind after commissioning Michelangelo to paint more of the Sistine Chapel twenty-four years after he had finished the ceiling.

After showering Anne with gifts, Henry popped the question. She said yes to the dress. It was too good to be true, which is usually a sign that it's not.

While the pope was dragging his feet, Henry's advisers tried to change his mind. Downgrading from Katherine of Aragon to Anne of Nowhere was a mistake. Besides the fact that Anne had no political connections like Katherine did to Spain, the people of England thought that Anne was a witch and had put a spell on Henry to make him marry her. And she wasn't acting like a joyful bride-to-be. She demanded all of Katherine's crown jewels, and began sending Katherine to smaller and smaller houses with fewer and fewer servants until she ended up living in an empty castle in a deserted town. Anne made Princess Mary, Henry and Katherine's daughter, give up her rights to the throne, and she demanded that Mary hold her train as she walked.

Henry was no picnic either.

Done waiting for the pope, Henry made himself the decider and his first decision was to give himself everything he wanted. Forget the pope and the Church of Rome. Henry was already king; now he'd start his own religion and be his own version of the pope in England.

It took six years to pull it off, but Anne Boleyn and Henry VIII got married on January 25, 1533. It was too bad the people of England hated Anne. Their first initials, *H* and *A*, were combined in showy displays that spelled HA! HA! And that's just what people did on her coronation day—they laughed at her.

Now it was Anne's turn to give Henry what she had promised: a son. She became pregnant right away. The birth announcements with the words "It's a boy" were prepared in advance. But then Anne gave birth to a girl. They called her Princess Elizabeth. The tournament and the fireworks planned by the king were canceled. Anne still wanted to wedge her new daughter ahead of Princess Mary, so Elizabeth would get first pick of the royal princes to marry. Princess Mary got downgraded to Lady Mary, and Anne took all of Lady Mary's jewels and gave them to Princess Elizabeth.

After they got married, it didn't take long for Henry to start seeing other women. Wives, even queens, were supposed to look the other way, but not Anne. She told him to quit it, and come home on time. She wasn't going to take any of his baloney.

Months after Anne was already the queen the pope finally made a decision: Henry should go back to Katherine of Aragon at once. Katherine waited for Henry to come get her; but though she got all dressed up she had nowhere to go.

Anne's second pregnancy ended in a stillbirth. The baby was dead.

Henry had more affairs with ladies-in-waiting, and whenever Anne knew the woman's identity, she'd banish her from court. At this rate, pretty soon it would be ladies-all-gone.

Their two years of marriage went from better to worse in record time. Henry had turned into a big blob with a nasty personality. And Anne hadn't kept her promise to produce a boy. As the years rolled by and in between her miscarriage, and two stillbirths, Anne advocated getting the Bible published in English instead of only in Latin, so people could understand what they were reading. Henry unleashed a reign of terror on churches and monasteries. The priests who didn't acknowledge him as the head of a new English church were disemboweled, decapitated, or slowly roasted to death.

History started to repeat itself on the castle (home) front. Henry was giving expensive gifts to the lady-in-waiting Jane Seymour, and Anne caught her sitting on his lap. A few days later Anne miscarried her last baby while Henry worked on getting rid of her. And he took their little daughter, Elizabeth, out of the order of succession. It was all so familiar. He hadn't changed at all. Anne figured he would send her away to some far-off place like he had done to his first wife. Little did she know, she was in for something much worse.

Out of the blue, five men were arrested. They were charged with treason, and with having intimate relations with the queen. The five innocent men were found guilty and sentenced to death.

Anne was brought to trial, accused of adultery, of conspiring to kill the king, and of laughing at his clothes and making fun of his poetry. She wasn't allowed to have a lawyer. Anne denied the charges.

The verdict was "guilty." She would be burned or beheaded. Henry VIII would decide. An English queen had never been put to death before. It was unimaginable.

On May 19, 1536, a crowd squeezed into the Tower courtyard. Anne wore a dark robe edged in fur with a long white cape. She climbed the scaffold with four of her ladies-in-waiting. She gave the headsman some money to ensure he'd do the job in one whack.

Before he got to work, Anne Boleyn gave a speech, hoping to save her life, saying that the king was a really great guy. Then she gathered her long hair in a cap so it wouldn't get in the way. She got down on her knees, and kept her hand on the cap because it was slipping. The headsman had removed his shoes and crept up behind her when she wasn't looking. He circled the sword above his head a couple of times and without her seeing it coming, he cut off her head with one swing. Anne Boleyn was dead at thirty-five years old.

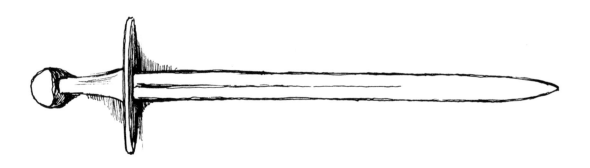

After the crowd dispersed, the four ladies-in-waiting put the matching pieces of Anne's corpse into a chest and covered them with a sheet—a whole new skill set for ladies-in-waiting to master. Those ladies got a good look at what could happen if you married the wrong person.

The very next day Henry VIII and Jane Seymour were engaged. What was she thinking?

Out of Henry VIII's six wives, three were ladies-in-waiting. One other lady eventually lost her head.

It took only one generation for Anne's daughter to learn the lesson that marrying the wrong person could kill you and that women *could* rule England. Anne Boleyn and Henry VIII's daughter, Elizabeth I, ruled England on her own for over forty-four years with her head safely on her neck. And since Elizabeth never found the right man to marry, she didn't see any reason to bother.

Anne Boleyn had taught Elizabeth by grisly example.

THE LINEUP OF UNLUCKY LADIES (THREE IN-WAITING)

1. Katherine of Aragon: arranged marriage, from Spain
2. **Anne Boleyn**: lady-in-waiting for Katherine of Aragon
3. Jane Seymour: lady-in-waiting for Katherine of Aragon and for Anne Boleyn
4. Anne of Cleves: arranged marriage, from Germany
5. Katherine Howard: lady-in-waiting for Anne of Cleves
6. Katherine Parr: lady at court

#2 AND #5 BEHEADED • #1 AND #4 DIVORCED
#3 DIED IN CHILDBIRTH • #6 WIDOWED

GOOD-BYE, CRUEL WORLD

SOME OF ANNE'S SPEECH, GIVEN moments before her beheading, May 19, 1536, at the Tower of London:

"I come here only to die, and thus to yield myself humbly to the will of the King, my lord. And if, in my life, I did ever offend the King's Grace, surely with my death I do now atone. I come hither to accuse no man, nor to speak anything of that whereof I am accused, as I know full well that aught I say in my defence doth not appertain to you. I pray and beseech you all, good friends, to pray for the life of the King, my sovereign lord and yours, who is one of the best princes on the face of the earth, who has always treated me so well that better could not be, wherefore I submit to death with good will, humbly asking pardon of all the world. If any person will meddle with my cause, I require them to judge the best. Thus I take my leave of the world, and of you, and I heartily desire you all to pray for me. . . . O Lord God, have pity on my soul! To Christ I commend my soul!"

ANNE'S PREGNANCY LOG

First pregnancy: daughter, Elizabeth, born
Second pregnancy: stillbirth at almost full term (full term is 40 weeks)
Third pregnancy: stillbirth at 6 months
Fourth pregnancy: miscarriage at 15 weeks

Stillbirth: when a lifeless baby is delivered
Miscarriage: when a pregnancy ends on its own within the first 20 weeks

It's possible that Anne Boleyn had Rh-negative blood, and that Henry had Rh-positive blood. Traces of Henry's Rh-positive blood could have entered Anne's bloodstream after her first pregnancy. She would then have been highly sensitive to Henry's blood. Subsequently, her following pregnancies would result in stillbirths and miscarriages. Anne Boleyn and Henry VIII would never have had another living child.

COOL FACT

King Henry VIII was actually to blame for all those female heirs.

Mothers always carry an X chromosome. It is the father's body that decides whether that X chromosome is going to combine with another X, making a girl, or with a Y, making a boy.

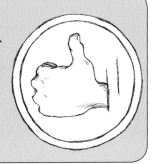

ARRESTED AND PUT TO DEATH

THESE MEN WERE ACCUSED OF having affairs with the queen and were duly beheaded two days before Anne.

Henry Norris • Sir Francis Weston • William Brereton • Mark Smeaton
George Boleyn, Viscount Rochford (her own brother)

ISAAC NEWTON

THE LAW'S IN TOWN

Scientist
Born: Lincolnshire, England,
January 4, 1643
Died: London, England,
March 31, 1727
84 years old

ISAAC NEWTON THOUGHT of the world as a big puzzle that he should solve. So while everybody else was minding their own business making friends and being loved by their families, Newton figured out why the sun and all the planets don't randomly float around and bang into each other, why the tides go in and out, and why a ball stays at rest until you kick it. He unscrambled things, gave them formulas, and turned them into laws. And he liked keeping them all to himself, because he really hated to share—or maybe he was never taught how. His scientific findings prove his genius, but the other half of Newton's life marked him as a notable whack job. His decision to drop science and become a crime-fighting manhunter qualify Isaac Newton as one of the biggest puzzles of all time.

Isaac Newton fell to earth in 1643. He didn't get his smarts by way of nurturing since his dad died before he was even born and his mom abandoned him when he was only three. She took off with a new husband and had three more kids someplace else while Newton was left with his grandmother on a farm only seven miles away. Newton threatened to burn his mother's new family home down and that sums up how he felt about that. Mom eventually came back with his three half siblings after  her second husband died, but then she sent Newton off to boarding school. He wasn't wanted by his mom and you don't need to be a scientist to know that can ruin a person, so it's hard to know the answer to the riddle of which came first: Newton *wanting* to be left alone or Newton *being* left alone.

At school, with no laws of socializing in his arsenal, Newton didn't play well with others, so he picked fights instead. When he wasn't fighting he was copying books—word for word—in neat, weensy, one-sixteenth-of-an-inch-high handwriting. Who needed friends or family anyway? He learned to have his own good time.

When school ended for Newton at sixteen, his mom demanded he come back home. Not because she missed him, but because she wanted him to work on the family farm: herding sheep, managing the workers, and figuring out how much to

charge for hay. If she'd known one iota about her son she'd have known that on the list of jobs Newton shouldn't do, people manager and farmer were at the top. So there were no sad good-byes nine months later when he packed a pound of candles, some ink, and a chamber pot (portable potty), and left for Trinity College at Cambridge University, a place where he would know more than anyone there could ever teach him.

A couple of times during his college years, Newton was forced to go back to the farm. Up to a thousand people a week were dropping like flies all over England because of the plague. Fleas sucked the blood of dead rats, then jumped onto people for more bloodsucking.

All this sucking spread the plague. Every public place was closed. Exiled back at the farm, there would be no more chores for Newton. He went off and did his own thing even though no one knew what that actually was. Whether he was staring at the sun or at the night sky, his head was always in the clouds.

And it wasn't as if Newton had a girlfriend to look at the moon with or any buddies to spitball ideas around with. He didn't share anything with his family either, because he knew they couldn't care less.

When he was finally able to return to Cambridge, he showed his math professor that he hadn't goofed off while school was closed for plague days. As a matter of fact, what Newton had done without input from anyone was so revolutionary he had surpassed his professor by a hundred light-years. Eventually, the professor handed Newton the keys to the school, his professorship, and his lab. Newton was twenty-seven years old.

Later, his ex-professor took Newton's work to the Royal Society in London, which was basically the first science club. Members would do experiments and prove things to each other. This so-called Scientific Revolution was fueled by brilliant thinkers sharing information so that they could build on each other's ideas to reach the next big idea more quickly. Two heads *are* better than one. For example, it took more than one person to think of luggage with wheels. Someone thought up the wheel and another person thought of the luggage part, and even that took a few thousand years. Anyway, people finally figured out that knowledge was power, and it was better when shared.

Everyone except Newton.

The Royal Society welcomed Newton into the club because they liked the way he proved his theory that the sun's white light wasn't an absence of color but a combination of *all* the colors. Think of an invisible rainbow. One thing led to the next, and Newton, using this idea, added a little mirror to a telescope. (That's how every telescope has been made ever since.) Newton demonstrated his cool telescope for the Society. But once there, Newton was reminded that he had already given up on people, and he didn't feel more loved or appreciated after divulging what he had figured out on his own. He was practically allergic to defending his "hypothesis." He hated it when others would say, "Oh, yeah, I

thought of that too." And Newton didn't bother to answer any of their ding-dong questions—really—he had figured it out already.

Newton escaped back to Cambridge without even telling them his best stuff. Like calculus, and his laws of gravity. He dragged his feet for a couple of decades before he divulged those. Several times, Newton would use another scientist's data, calculate a new formula, and make it a law, but he didn't acknowledge the other person's input. He liked the scientific world the way it already worked—in secrecy—every man for himself. He wouldn't share and he wasn't interested in the day-to-day discoveries of the Scientific Revolution that he happened to be a big part of.

Just when he should've been collaborating and expanding his thinking, he dove back into the science of the Middle Ages, abandoning his most precious commodity—his own mind. Maybe it was just a good excuse to get away from people, but the bizarre nature of his next obsession boggles even lesser minds. Or maybe it was just greed. Newton wanted to turn lead into gold—a process called alchemy.

Also called witchcraft, magic, and pretend science, but there was one thing everybody called it—illegal. It was a get-rich-quick scheme of conmen and counterfeiters. The Act Against Multipliers from the 1400s had outlawed the making of gold by alchemy, because then all the wrong people would get rich. On the sly (except for the billowing smoke and fumes emanating from his lab), Newton distilled, heated, and fermented concoctions of mercury, lead, and arsenic, attempting to make gold. And he didn't just dabble, he did it on and off for twenty-five years.

Decades' worth of recipes, and over a million tiny squished words, filled his papers with meticulously measured brews that he touched, tasted, and inhaled. While he scribbled and stirred, Newton's sharp mind grew foggy with symptoms of toxic lead and mercury poisoning: depression, anxiety, insomnia, loss of appetite and memory—until he finally collapsed. Isaac Newton's brain was in a muddle. He was fifty years old.

Something else in England had also collapsed—the monetary system. Almost 95 percent of the coins in circulation were counterfeit. Crooks melted silver and diluted it with lesser metals, which was a distant version of what Newton had been attempting for quite some time. Men caught defacing money were hanged and women were burned at the stake. Luckily, Newton managed to keep his illegal obsession a secret, but it was no secret that he was the smartest man in England, so in 1696 he was asked to be warden of the mint, where all the money was made.

Newton wasn't a joiner, and his sanity was at stake, but he still took the job at the Tower of London—a place of beheadings, imprisonments, and buildings with names like the Bloody Tower, in a city where half a million strangers were jammed together without plumbing. In London, his new home, the death rate exceeded the birthrate. The toxic and confirmed people-hater who had barely recovered from losing his marbles dusted off his limited people skills and his math abilities and showed up for work.

Newton studied two hundred years of England's accounts, organized assembly lines, created schedules for five hundred workers and fifty horses, and recoined all the money in England in two years.

Another puzzle solved.

But there was more to Newton's job as warden of the mint—hunting down counterfeiters and enforcing the law. There wasn't anything to study or decode. Police didn't start keeping records of crimes or criminals until 1829. He had figured out the behavior of bodies in motion, but *not* that of living, breathing bodies in motion. The people puzzle still bewildered him, and he judged everybody the same way: he didn't like them. Talk to people? What use was that?

With zero skills as a crime fighter, and his laws of gravity, motion, tides, and all the rest far behind him, now Newton *was* the law. He was definitely the only member of the Royal Society who ever followed criminal leads, spied on people, and issued arrest warrants. And in Newtonian style, he started writing lots and lots of crazy notes. He also *had* to make friends in this job; they just happened to be thieves, extortionists, and thugs. He conspired with them to entrap counterfeiters and throw them in prison.

Newgate, an overcrowded prison with a sewer running through it, had no beds and little food. It was a death sentence itself; more people died there waiting for trial than on the gallows. Newton grilled inmates, dragging men out of their cells and into the narrow hallways. Then he'd bribe and terrorize them until they confessed and signed testimonies. Being shackled in irons or being forced to squeal by the greatest thinker of the time didn't make it any less awful. It was worse. Newton vented the rage he had for his fellow man in his scribbled, crossed-out, ink-blobbed rants. The distance between him and everyone else had been widened and confirmed.

Hundreds of interrogations and twenty-four hangings later, Newton's three-and-a-half-year reign as warden of the mint was over. Before moving on to his next job as master of the mint, he burned all of his interrogation records. In his entire life, these were the *only* papers he destroyed. Dark invisible forces were raging inside Isaac Newton and in those papers, and he wanted to keep them a secret. On the outside, he appeared sane and in control, as can be seen in the more than fourteen portraits he commissioned of himself during his time in London. But on the inside, he was a loveless man, a predictable outcome for the victim of a loveless life.

He lacked in love, but he had plenty of money. As master of the mint, Newton received a percentage of every English pound (England's money, like the US dollar) produced. He had finally found a way to make gold after all. He held that job until his death in 1727, at eighty-four years old.

In 1872, his alchemy papers were offered as a gift to the Cambridge University Library by the descendants of Newton's half niece Catherine Barton, who had kept the papers after he died. But the university didn't want them. Later, John Maynard Keynes, the world-renowned economist, bought them. He said, "They have, beyond doubt, no substantial value whatever except as a fascinating sidelight on the mind of our greatest genius. . . . He was the last of the magicians."

In 1979, a lock of Newton's hair was analyzed. It contained large amounts of mercury as well as lead. High levels of lead are known to cause violent behavior.

The two pieces of Isaac Newton's life don't fit together: the superstar scientist and philosopher, and the crime-fighting manhunter. We may never unravel the invisible laws that were working inside his mind and in his heart, or the riddle of why he tried to turn metal into gold for so many years of his life. But why he turned on his fellow man might be the easier piece to decipher. Like the Beatles song title "All You Need Is Love," and Isaac Newton never got any.

NEWTON'S BIG IDEAS

1. Three laws of motion: inertia, acceleration, and action and reaction
2. Law of universal gravitation
3. Reflecting telescope
4. Calculus, originally called the fluxions
5. White light is all the colors, circular color wheel thingy

NEWTON'S SINS

A few misdeeds from Newton's 1662 list:

- Making a mousetrap on Thy day
- Squirting water on Thy day
- Threatning my father and mother Smith to burne them and the house over them
- Wishing death and hoping it to some
- Striking many
- Stealing cherry cobs from Eduard Storer
- Denying that I did so
- Denying a crossbow to my mother and grandmother though I knew of it
- Punching my sister
- Robbing my mothers box of plums and sugar

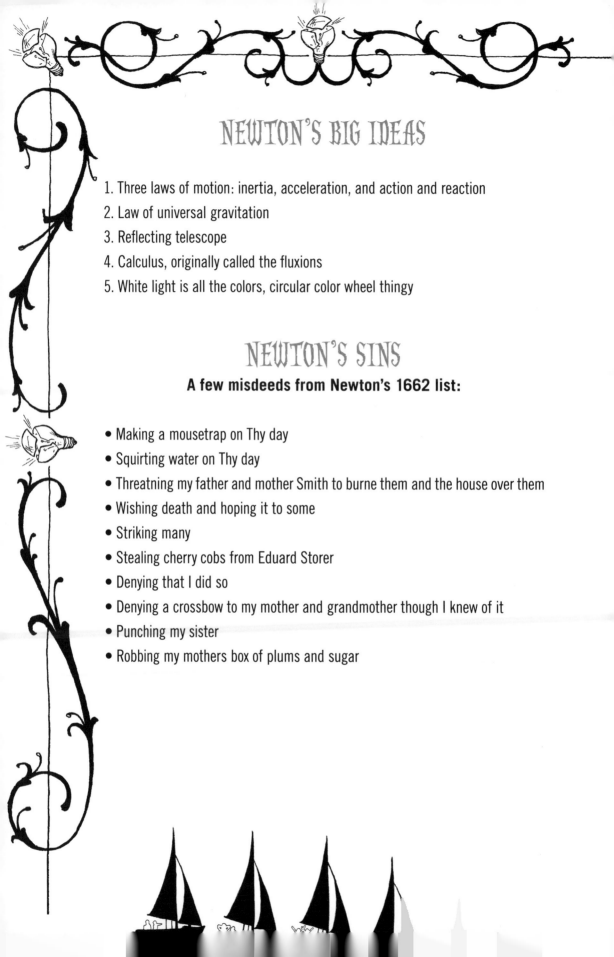

SCIENTIFIC REVOLUTION

THE SCIENTIFIC REVOLUTION WAS THE ERA when reason began to surpass religion as a basis for studying the world at large.

OTHERS WHO HAD BIG IDEAS

- NICOLAUS COPERNICUS: planets revolve around the sun
- JOHANNES KEPLER: planets revolve in an elliptical pattern
- GALILEO GALILEI: telescope, *and* Earth rotates on its axis
- FRANCIS BACON: scientific method—only with slow, faithful work will answers be found

NEWTON'S BIG SECRET

AFTER HE DIED, NEWTON'S RELATIVES concealed most of his writings on religion and alchemy because they could have severely damaged his scientific reputation. Most of these papers became available to scholars only when they were released on microfilm in 1991.

THEORY OF GRAVITY

IN CALCULUS

$$F = G \frac{mM}{r^2}$$

BENEDICT ARNOLD

STINKER, TRAITOR, SOLDIER, SPY

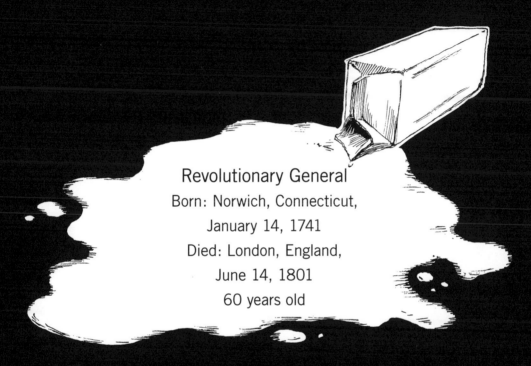

Revolutionary General
Born: Norwich, Connecticut,
January 14, 1741
Died: London, England,
June 14, 1801
60 years old

BENEDICT ARNOLD WAS madly in love with one person—himself. And he did not take criticism well. He thought it was okay to lie, spy, cheat, loot, and go behind friends' backs. If he was called out on his crummy behavior, he'd never apologize. Instead, he'd stage a grown-up version of a temper tantrum. Truth and loyalty meant nothing to him. He had to be the first, the richest, and the most important—putting titles before his name, like Doctor and Brigadier General because he thought he was better than everybody else. He was so greedy he sold out George Washington, the father of our country, for a million dollars. Mr. B. A. betrayed America so badly that three hundred years later, when you think of a traitor, the first and only name that comes to mind is Benedict Arnold.

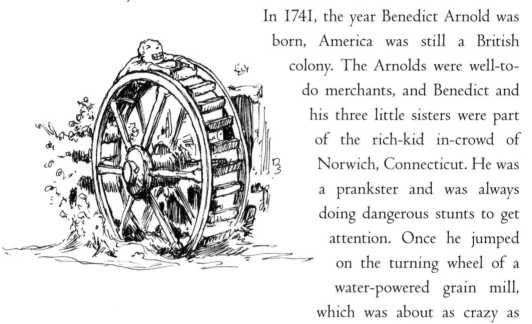

In 1741, the year Benedict Arnold was born, America was still a British colony. The Arnolds were well-to-do merchants, and Benedict and his three little sisters were part of the rich-kid in-crowd of Norwich, Connecticut. He was a prankster and was always doing dangerous stunts to get attention. Once he jumped on the turning wheel of a water-powered grain mill, which was about as crazy as hopping onto a moving Ferris wheel. And while he was at boarding school learning how to act rich and entitled, he was also wowing fellow students by doing things like prancing around on top of a burning barn. Meanwhile, back at home, things were falling apart. Two of his sisters died of yellow fever. Then his dad lost his shipping business and couldn't pay Benedict's expensive tuition anymore. Benedict had to drop out and return home.

The once hoity-toity Arnolds lost everything, Dad became a drunk, and thirteen-year-old Benedict joined a gang of lower-class boys. Benedict was full of ideas for stealing things and starting fires—whatever it took to draw the biggest crowd. Once the whole

town watched him fight the authorities. Another time, he shot off a cannon—almost blowing off his own head. He also fired a gun at a man dating his sister.

Trying to nip his bad behavior in the bud, his mom signed Benedict into the legal custody of her still-wealthy relatives. Leaving his struggling family behind in squalor didn't bother Benedict; he got to live in a mansion again, so he didn't mind being exiled.

Benedict had straightened up enough by the time he was twenty-one to have his own herb and medicine business. But he was already a man who couldn't be trusted.

He called himself "Doctor Arnold from London," even though he wasn't a doctor and wasn't from London. His store sign read: FOR HIMSELF AND FOR EVERYONE. What he really meant was "For Me and for Me." He wasn't paying his bills, and it got to the point where Benedict owed people hundreds of thousands of dollars.

At that time, colonial Americans were fighting for life, liberty, and the pursuit of happiness. For Benedict, the pursuit of happiness meant one thing—making a lot of money. But the British were heavily taxing American businesses. To avoid paying, Benedict cheated. When a British officer caught him smuggling, Benedict beat the officer to a pulp, then tied him to a post and whipped him. Arnold was prosecuted for the crime, but he didn't even show up for his own trial. He just wrote an article about himself for the local newspaper. It didn't hurt that Benedict was about to marry the sheriff's daughter, Margaret Mansfield, and start a family with her.

Motivated by his desire for wealth and to avoid taxes, Benedict became the leader of a secret group, the Sons of Liberty, made up of shopkeepers and tradesmen. They tarred and feathered folks loyal to the British king. Then, as the captain of the local militia, Benedict and his men illegally helped themselves to all the guns and ammo in the colony's weapon warehouse.

He was a nasty fellow with a short fuse, but he also showed leadership, which worked to his advantage when fighting Tories, the Americans who sided with the British during the American Revolutionary War. In no time, he became Colonel Benedict Arnold, then brigadier general, and then Commander of the Lakes (Lake Champlain). He led America's first offensive attack ever at Fort Ticonderoga; its first foreign invasion in Quebec, Canada; and he was in charge of the first naval fleet. Orders are orders, except most of the things Benedict achieved happened when he wasn't following them. He was a quick-decision man to a fault. And if someone crossed him, he'd crack open his head.

Benedict was brave, and he accomplished a lot of firsts, but he was a regular nightmare. He looted the Canadian city of Montreal and pretended he didn't. He always denied wrongdoing, and he demanded credit for everything good. When he wasn't promoted to major general because he never obeyed his superiors, he went whining and complaining to Commander George Washington, the only person who could open any doors at this point for the out-of-control Benedict Arnold. Washington felt sorry for Arnold because he had seriously wounded his leg while fighting for American independence, and his wife had recently died. So Washington gave Arnold a second chance, appointing him military governor of Philadelphia. It was a cushy job: What could go wrong? He warned Benedict to try to be "most effectual, and at the same time least offensive."

Except his behavior was most offensive and least effectual. Benedict moved into a mansion, hired a big staff, and rode around Philly in a fancy carriage—just how he liked it.

Nobody else liked it.

In his new city, Benedict started hanging out with Tories, the very people he and Washington had been fighting against for years! He even married a Tory named Peggy Shippen.

Then, to the huge embarrassment of Washington, Benedict Arnold was court-martialed on eight counts of swiping government funds, illegal use of public property, and being disrespectful to just about everybody. Benedict represented himself in court because no lawyer could quite state his case the way he could. What he mostly needed to clarify was that he really, really deserved more money. Benedict was so pleased with his performance, he had the 179-page court record printed in two languages and distributed in America and in Europe.

Even though he was as guilty as sin, Benedict got off easy. Lucky to have dodged prison, he still wasn't satisfied. He went grumbling to his pal Washington asking for a full pardon.

Being the nice guy that he was, or maybe because he just didn't want to see the obvious, Washington offered Benedict a third chance to redeem himself. He asked Benedict to fight alongside him in a forthcoming battle. But there was no pleasing Benedict Arnold. Staring redemption and a chance for glory in the face, what did Benedict do? He blew it big-time. And no surprise: going to the dark side came with a hefty paycheck.

Benedict talked Washington into giving him command of the fort at West Point, along the Hudson River.

Even though he promised to repair the damaged fort, retrain the men, and patch up the chain that stretched across the Hudson to block the passage of British ships, he did the opposite. But that was nothing compared to Arnold sending classified information to the enemy via his wife. Arnold was going to hand over the fort to the British.

If his plan to overthrow West Point was a success, Benedict would get 20,000 British pounds (about 3.4 million dollars in today's money). Even if the plan failed, Benedict wanted 10,000 pounds, but the British would only agree to pay 6,000 pounds.

Benedict Arnold met in secret with a British major named John

André, and they wrote up the plans for seizing the fort. The plot was panning out even better than originally imagined: George Washington would be at the fort in a couple of days. Just think how much money the British would pay if he captured Washington!

What happened in the next forty-eight hours was an epic farce. Whatever could go wrong went wrong, starting with Major André getting caught with the secret plans in his boots. The plans were then sent to George Washington's headquarters, but Washington had already left for breakfast at Benedict's (maybe for eggs). Not knowing that Benedict had written the plans to capture the fort, Washington's officers sent the papers to Benedict's house, but they arrived before Washington did. Benedict saddled a horse and split two minutes later. Washington had breakfast without Benedict and had a disturbing meeting with Benedict's nervous wife, who was acting nuts and needy to give her guilty husband more time to escape.

Washington headed to West Point where the secret spy papers finally got to him, and that's when Washington understood Arnold's treasonous plans to help the British capture the fort.

The gig was up for Benedict Arnold, but he had escaped. He got on board a British ship anchored up the Hudson. No one even thought to arrest his accomplice/wife. And once again, Benedict

Arnold got another fancy title. This time it was brigadier general in the British army.

Washington took it hard. He ordered Major André hanged for treason a few days later. Benedict Arnold never even spent a single night in jail. As a British officer, he later attacked cities in Virginia, and even New London, Connecticut, only twelve miles from his hometown. He burned the whole town to the ground.

The British lost the Revolutionary War, and Benedict Arnold hightailed it to London. Nobody there liked him either, because nobody likes a traitor, even when he's on your side.

Never happy with the 6,000 pounds he received for his failed takeover of West Point, Benedict kept nagging the British for the full 10,000 until the day he died. Even after all his complaining about money, Benedict Arnold made more money than any other American officer in the American Revolution.

He had been a greedy liar and a bully. He made the equivalent of about a million dollars and was never punished for his crimes, but it's hard to think of a bigger failure than Benedict Arnold. For pure, all-around untrustworthiness, Benedict Arnold is your man. If your word is no good—you are nothing. As the master of his own disaster he secured his last and final title: Traitor Benedict Arnold.

Whatever you do in life, remember: don't be a Benedict Arnold.

WHO'S WHO IN THE AMERICAN REVOLUTION

AMERICAN SIDE

Patriots
Whigs
Rebels
Blue Coats
Continental Army
Revolutionaries
Militia

BRITISH SIDE

Loyalists
Tories
The King's Men
Red Coats
British Army

U.S. CONSTITUTION

TREASON: ARTICLE III, SECTION 3

"Treason against the United States, shall consist only in levying War against them, or in adhering to their Enemies, giving them Aid and Comfort. No Person shall be convicted of Treason unless on the Testimony of two Witnesses to the same overt Act, or on Confession in open Court.

The Congress shall have Power to declare the Punishment of Treason, but no Attainder of Treason shall work Corruption of Blood, or Forfeiture except during the Life of the Person attainted."

If Benedict Arnold had been captured, he would have been hanged for treason. Arnold escaped to England at the end of the war. After failing at business there, he set up a store in Canada. A few years later, it burned down. When he tried

to collect the insurance money, he was denied. Even his own business partner figured Benedict had set the fire just to get the money. He moved back to England.

BENEDICT ARNOLD'S WIVES AND KIDS

WIFE	CHILDREN	BORN
Margaret Mansfield	Benedict	America
	Richard	America
	Henry	America
Peggy Shippen	Edward	America
	James Robertson	America
	Margaret	England
	George	England
	Sophia	England
	George	England
	William Fitch	England

ALL IN THE FAMILY

OVER IN ENGLAND, BENEDICT WAS constantly hustling to get more money. He got his three eldest sons in on a money scheme. Thirteen-year-old Benedict was commissioned as a British ensign. Twelve-year-old Richard and nine-year-old Henry both became lieutenants in Dad's regiment. Even though they didn't serve until they got older, all three got paid salaries right away.

SUSAN B. ANTHONY

VOTER REVOLT

American Suffragist
Born: Adams, Massachusetts,
February 15, 1820
Died: Rochester, New York,
March 13, 1906
86 years old

IMAGINE LIVING TODAY in Pakistan or Saudi Arabia, where women can't vote or own property, can't get an education, a divorce, or equal pay; where being beaten by your husband is okay; and where women can't speak out without being terrorized. Susan B. Anthony was born in a country like that—the United States. In 1820, one-half of the population in America had as few rights as a potted plant. The other half, men, liked it that way. Women were trained not to complain about it or disagree. But then along came Susan B. Anthony. She wouldn't keep her mouth shut about it. We've all said, "But it's not fair!" for something or other, but Susan said it once and then she couldn't stop. Fair was fair, and there was

no room for compromise. No amount of belittling, hate mail, or angry mobs could stop this pioneering pain in the butt from her dedication to getting women their equal share of rights—and the vote—as citizens of the United States. Except she herself never got it.

Susan was number two of seven siblings born into a traditional Quaker household.

She didn't have to worry about sharing her toys and games with her brothers and sisters since Quakers didn't allow them. They lived by the words of the famous Quaker prayer: *'Tis the gift to be simple, 'tis the gift to be free, 'Tis the gift to come down where we ought to be, And when we find ourselves in the place just right, 'Twill be in the valley of love and delight.* The main delight Susan enjoyed was reverence for the Lord, which came with no singing (unless it was slow), no dancing (especially not slow), and no art. Susan had a frill-free childhood of plain talk, gray dresses, and endless chores, thanks to the eleven of her dad's mill employees living at her house. But underneath that gray dress that

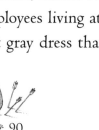

looked like a piece of concrete with a hat on top, some serious rebellion was brewing.

Meanwhile, all she did when she wasn't at school was help her mom cook and clean. Her male schoolteacher wouldn't allow her to learn long division because it was thought that if a girl used her brain too much her baby-making parts would die. Susan embraced the core Quaker idea that everything must flow from what one experienced. And she definitely knew what her teacher said was wrong. Eventually, Susan went off to boarding school where all she mastered was how to perfectly dot her *i*'s. Yet Susan became a teacher too, eventually running a school herself. By then, her dad had given up the mill to become a teacher. Susan made only one-quarter of what her dad earned, and only half of what her teacher brother earned. No wonder they didn't want women to learn math.

Out on her own, away from the Quakers, Susan became less Quaker-ly, dropping the plain talk of "thee" and "thou," and getting herself plaid dresses, bonnets, and dates to some dances. What she didn't like at the dances was men drinking, because drunk men often went home and beat their wives and kids. If these women wanted to get away from their abusive husbands, it was illegal to take their kids with them. And since any money or property they owned belonged to their husband, the women were usually trapped. But Susan wasn't, and she spoke up about it on their behalf.

Hardly anyone was ready to listen to a spinster advocating that women leave their husbands. Most people thought women— especially Susan, with her radical ideas—were to be seen and not heard. Men saw no reason to change the model of "what's mine is mine" and "what's yours is mine too." The completely slanted male press called her a "shrieking shrew." But Susan was just getting started; fighting to ban alcohol grew into something she really wanted to blab about, women's rights. The difficulty of changing peoples' minds about women's place in society was practically insurmountable back then. And for this Anthony needed sensible flat boots on the ground. Along with Elizabeth Cady Stanton and a team of other women, she started a women's uprising, the women's suffrage movement, out of nothing but their wits and their voices. Without the Internet or anything else with a wire attached to it, the only way to get out the message was to meet and greet, talking it up with everyone they saw. And to see as many people as they could, they had to get moving. Elizabeth Cady Stanton had seven children, so she was a tad distracted. Susan B. Anthony never married, designating her the one who packed her bags and went around trying to improve women's lives.

She traveled in trains, open buggies, and sleighs circulating petitions, holding meetings, and going door-to-door. Her message: Women should be allowed to own property. Wake up! Women are not doormats, and now's the time to stop acting like it. Both men and women behaved rudely when they heard that, and they slammed doors in her face, and jeered and ridiculed her, but she kept going—renting halls and giving speeches.

Some people couldn't wait for her to catch the next wagon out of town. A woman speaking in public was considered crass, not to mention all that thinking she was doing while her baby-making parts died right in front of everybody. Those who stayed and heard Susan's resolve for equality in her clear, musical voice were moved by her good sense, heart, and charisma. But then some would throw fruit at her. It didn't matter if one person or three hundred showed up. She had the simple yet bothersome truth to tell them: the way women were treated wasn't fair.

Along with the inequality of women, the other most unfair thing in America was slavery. Susan became active in the antislavery movement too. The abolitionists put Anthony's organizing talents and her never-give-up attitude to work. People sat with pistols in their laps, but that didn't stop her. She got men elected to Congress who would vote for the Thirteenth Amendment to the Constitution to abolish slavery. But then no one helped her in return. The politicians didn't lift a finger, sticking the word "male" in the Fourteenth Amendment that gave the right to vote to all citizens. That one word meant half the population was left out. The politicians had used her to get elected, but deep down they considered women's causes deadweight. They got men their rights and nothing more. And they wanted Anthony to zip it up and go home and bake something.

So Susan B. Anthony and her women's rights were left in limbo. It was enough to make anyone else give up and go home. But Anthony couldn't. Women were taxed, imprisoned, and hanged just like men;

how could they be excluded from voting? It wasn't fair. And why wouldn't anyone listen?

That was when Anthony took action in a way that everyone was sure to hear about. It wasn't another meeting or conference or informative flyer. This time she simply broke the law by registering to vote. But not really. The law said "citizens" had the privilege of voting, so she believed she had every right to do it.

On November 5, 1872, Anthony and fourteen other women voted. Nine days later, a U.S. marshal casually told her to come down to the office whenever it was convenient for her. She asked, "Is this the way you arrest men?" She even wanted to be handcuffed, but the marshal wouldn't do it. They asked her dumb questions, like was she dressed like a man when she voted? Refusing to post bail, Susan hoped to be put in jail so she could claim illegal imprisonment and take her case all the way to the Supreme Court. But they wouldn't put her in jail.

At her trial, on June 17, 1873, *The United States of America v. Susan B. Anthony,* she wasn't expecting to be judged by a jury of her peers—it was a roomful of men in suits. Women weren't allowed to be on a

jury or to be admitted to the bar, so they couldn't be lawyers or judges either.

Her attorney called her as a witness, but the judge declared that Susan B. Anthony was incompetent as a witness because she was a woman. Say what? Then the judge told the jury that Anthony was guilty. And that was that.

Susan B. Anthony didn't have a chance. She didn't have to pay the fine or go to jail. But they did imprison the three men who had registered her to vote.

She had failed: "I am feeling today that life doesn't pay—the way seems so blocked up to me on all sides." But that feeling didn't stop her. Anthony kept on failing for thirty-three more years, fighting for women's right to vote. Anthony died in 1906. Women didn't get the right to vote for fourteen more years after that. It took thousands of women suffragettes marching in the streets to demonstrate that one person can make a difference, and so can one vote.

Susan B. Anthony cared little about her own comforts or personal rewards. Her radical idea that rights for women would transform everything for the better was way ahead of its time. Without equal rights, a country will not be a strong one, nor a wealthy and peaceful one. Nothing is more revolutionary than fairness and kindness, and the belief that human beings are linked but should not be ranked.

In her lifetime, she failed to see her ultimate goal achieved—women voting. But it was the United States government that failed *her*. She saw the good that was possible for humankind long before humankind caught up with her. And there is still more work to do.

When she said, "Failure is impossible," Susan B. Anthony did what everyone should do after failing: she didn't give up.

PROFILES OF GREAT WOMEN BORN IN THE 1820S

WAS IT SOMETHING IN THE WATER? OR WAS IT JUST TIME TO WAKE UP?

CLARA BARTON	HARRIET TUBMAN	FLORENCE NIGHTINGALE	SUSAN B. ANTHONY
BORN: 1821 First president of American Red Cross	**BORN:** ca. 1822 First American woman to lead armed assault	**BORN:** 1820 First school of nursing	**BORN:** 1820 First to vote
NICKNAME: Angel of the Battlefield	**NICKNAME:** Moses	**NICKNAME:** The Lady with the Lamp	**NICKNAME:** Sue
Wore long dresses and hair up	Wore long dresses and hair up	Wore long dresses and hair up	Wore long dresses and hair up
Had 0 children	Had 0 children of her own; adopted daughter	Had 0 children	Had 0 children
DIED: 1912 90 years old	**DIED:** 1913 90-ish years old	**DIED:** 1910 90 years old	**DIED:** 1906 86 years old

JURY DUTY

UNTIL 1979, WOMEN COULD SIMPLY opt out of jury duty if they didn't feel like participating. In 1979, Ruth Bader Ginsburg successfully argued before the Supreme Court that this practice was not fair to those on trial, who have the right to be tried by a jury of their peers. Up until this point, a woman on trial could easily have had a jury composed only of men.

WOMEN'S FIRSTS

- **1849** Elizabeth Blackwell is the first woman doctor.
- **1911** Marie Curie wins the Nobel Prize.
- **1916** Jeannette Rankin is elected to the U.S. House of Representatives.
- **1921** Edith Wharton wins the Pulitzer Prize for fiction.
- **1933** Frances Perkins is the first woman in a presidential cabinet.
- **1950** Harvard Law School admits women for the first time.
- **1963** Russian cosmonaut Valentina Tereshkova is the first woman in space.
- **1970** Diane Crump is the first woman jockey in the Kentucky Derby.
- **1979** Margaret Thatcher is elected prime minister of Great Britain.
- **1981** Sandra Day O'Connor is the first woman Supreme Court Justice.
- **1983** Sally Ride is the first U.S. woman in space.
- **1993** Janet Reno is the first female U.S. Attorney General.
- **2008** General Ann Dunwoody is the first woman to serve as a four-star general in the U.S. army.
- **2010** Katherine Bigelow wins Best Director at the Academy Awards.

NOT-SO-COOL FACTS

- **Worldwide, women perform 66 percent of the work, but they receive only 11 percent of the world's income.**
- Women still make less money than men. Exactly how much less is debatable, but the fact is that they get paid less to do the same work.
- **Women own only 1 percent of the world's land.**
- Population-wise, women beat men by 6 million.
- **60 percent of the kids who are not in school are girls.**

GEORGE
ARMSTRONG CUSTER

DRESSED TO KILL

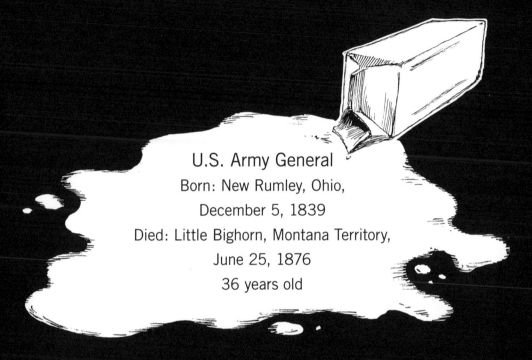

U.S. Army General
Born: New Rumley, Ohio,
December 5, 1839
Died: Little Bighorn, Montana Territory,
June 25, 1876
36 years old

GEORGE ARMSTRONG CUSTER was a bloodthirsty glory hound who feared nothing—except having to work a job where he couldn't kill people. Fame on the battlefield as general in the U.S. army is what he lived for, first in the Civil War, and then right after, fighting Native American Indians (plus, he loved the uniform). Brave to a fault, he'd charge into battle wearing his "hey, look at me" outfit with the gold embellishments, gauntlet gloves, and red tie, while his backup band played his theme song, "Garryowen." He just needed a target and off he'd go, guns a-blazing, wasting people left and right. Then he'd go home and get a glamour photo taken of himself. Custer was a quick-decision hit man who didn't try to

When our band plays "Garryowen"

figure anything out in advance, preferring to take wild risks while leading devoted soldiers and a few family members to their deaths.

Custer always knew how to make an entrance. Even his birth was a miracle to his parents because he was their first child to live after two older sons had died soon after they were born. This turned out to be the first of many celebrated survivals to come, and the start of the legendary "Custer's luck." His dad took him to volunteer militia meetings, and as he marched along with his toy musket, Custer knew following in his father's footsteps was all he wanted. After his three younger brothers and a sister were born, Custer got his first little army. He grew to be athletic and tall with boyish handsomeness, which helped him with his favorite hobby: conquering women.

One father didn't like Custer hanging out with his daughter, so he got rid of him by muscling through Custer's admission to the coveted U.S. Military Academy at West Point, which usually required top grades or the right connections to get in. Except for the discipline, the drills, and the rules, Custer excelled at hanging out with a bunch of guys playing army. Preferring to read romance novels instead of military code books, he was remembered for having the worst grades in the class, the most demerits, and the messiest room. Custer was also known for being late and inattentive, but at least he looked "pretty" while messing up. And he liked wearing costumes to act out poems, which his classmates called his "little freaks."

When the American Civil War began, Custer's class broke up; half joined the Southern Confederate side and the other half, including Custer, joined the Northern Union Army. Before long, ex–school chums got to use their newfound knowledge to aim guns at each other. Custer's army service was delayed because of his court-martial for failing to break up a fight when he was officer of the day. Custer's lowest grade was in cavalry tactics, but he was assigned to the cavalry anyway. His posting really didn't matter because all he'd be expected to do was line up on some mangy pony and get killed like everybody else. Before he galloped to war, he stopped in New York and bought a frock coat, jersey pants, a black slouch hat, and a maroon sash.

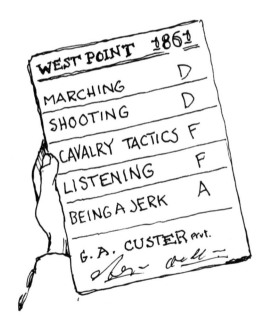

With gutsy bravado, Custer volunteered for every dangerous battle and scouting mission that he could, and it got so he couldn't stop. There he was at the Battle of Bull Run, at Gettysburg, and at Appomattox. Surviving heroic and flashy derring-do killing raids was a good reason to move him up in the ranks to temporary major general in the U.S. Army. And he got himself a theme song. He ran the Michigan brigade with such personal panache no one bothered to mention that more men died on his watch than in any other similar brigade in the Union. But heck, he got such great press, he made everyone look good around him (except the dead people).

You-know-who looked so especially fabulous that the press didn't mention the time Custer hunted a Confederate soldier and murdered him in cold blood because he wanted the man's thoroughbred horse, fancy saddle, and sword.

Custer found the time to marry Elizabeth Bacon. With his war record, the lucky lady had to figure that growing old with Custer would be a long shot. But she knew that he was as crazy in love with her as he was with battle, because he wrote her lovey-dovey twenty-page letters before heading off to slaughter people.

Custer's luck kept him from being one of the seven hundred fifty thousand Civil War deaths. Unlike everyone else who was tired of war, Custer wasn't. He started flogging his men for disobedience, and he killed them if they tried to leave the army. Slaying the enemy was one thing, but now Custer wanted to kill whoever was around. Luckily for his men, Custer was moving on to his next glory gig—the legalized murder of a whole race of people, Native American Indians. Any Indian he found outside a reservation was fair game.

His temporary general's rank was dropped

to lieutenant colonel, but a title or a righteous cause wasn't necessary. All Custer needed was a double-breasted buffalo coat and a matching buffalo-fur hat so he'd look good out on the Western plains. He arrived out West blind to the reality that the Indians liked their lives just the way they were and would fight to protect their families and their way of life.

Custer, basically a peacock with a pistol, would be leading the weakened U.S. cavalry against strong leaders like Sitting Bull and Crazy Horse, and their warriors who were fighting for their very existence. By the 1870s, there were only twenty-five thousand enlisted men left in the cavalry. Most were worthless dregs of society and criminals; 10 percent of them even registered under a fake name. It was up to the trigger-happy Custer, with fading charisma and a desire for mayhem, to turn six hundred and sixty of them into an effective fighting force.

Custer's wife, Elizabeth, joined him at remote forts in cold isolated places like Kansas and North Dakota while Custer made the frontier safe for gold diggers, railroad crews, and saloon owners. He'd go searching for Indians, but they were hard to find and weren't interested in facing off in battles, which Custer really missed doing. Frustrated after *not* finding any Indians for months on end out in the middle of nowhere, he left some men and his post, and selfishly dragged seventy-six troopers along with him on a fifty-seven-hour ride so he could spend a cozy night with his wife, something he'd shoot his own men for doing.

Custer was court-martialed for it. Punished with a year out of the service, Custer was reduced to writing about his exploits, instead of actually doing them, in his autobiography, *My Life on the Plains*. His fertile imagination surprised fellow military personnel so much many called it *My Lie on the Plains*.

But the sad truth was the military needed fearlessly devoted men like Custer to do the nasty job of murdering American Indians. Before the year was up, Custer was called back to his command—relieving Major Elliot, who had covered for him, because Custer's particular awfulness was needed at the Battle of the Washita.

The peace-loving Cheyenne leader Black Kettle did all he could to please the white man, and he was actually *on* a reservation when Custer ambushed his sleeping village. Of the one hundred and three killed, only eleven were warriors. Custer burned the Indian village, corralled the tribe's eight hundred horses, and massacred all of them too. Making sure Major Elliot wouldn't be taking over *his* regiment ever again, Custer abandoned him and eighteen of his men too. And Custer didn't retrieve their dead bodies either. Finally, the army saw Custer as the warped white man that he was.

Then, taking fifty-three Indian women hostage all winter long, Custer and his men did more things that no man would be proud of. The only thing Custer should have been wearing was stripes, in a place with bars on the windows. But the lines in his theme song were all so true: "where're we go they dread the name," and "for debt no man shall go to jail."

It's likely that the only soldiers in the Seventh Cavalry who still had any faith in Custer were his two younger brothers, his brother-in-law, and a nephew, who were his inner circle among the troops. And while Custer waited years for more action he learned taxidermy, researched Napoleon's tactics, and imitated his hand-in-the-shirt pose in a photo shoot. One winter in New York, he watched Shakespeare's play *Julius Caesar* forty times. It's not *that* good.

Finally, Custer received a mission for the Seventh Cavalry, which he called "the best cavalry in Uncle Sam's service," except it wasn't. Of the six hundred men, most had not fought anyone for three years, much less Lakota Sioux. No one had practiced shooting a gun while bouncing up and down on a horse, which is what they'd be doing. Probably pretending he was Caesar celebrating his battle triumphs in a big spectacle, Custer took the Seventh Cavalry prancing in a parade out of the fort to go kill Indians at Little Bighorn.

Several regiments, including Custer's, advanced from different directions and were ordered to meet up at the Indian camp so they could participate in a combined coordinated attack. Custer's first big mistake was separating his company into four smaller groups before assessing the enemy's numbers or planning exactly where he was going. He peeled off with his agile group of two-hundred-plus men so he could arrive first and start shooting. Custer marched his men for about thirty-four hours straight, from 5:00 a.m. on one day to 3:00 p.m. the next. His scouts advised him that there were more Indians than anyone had ever seen, six to eight thousand, and that they didn't have enough bullets to shoot them all. Believing he was bulletproof, the only thing Custer worried about was missing his chance for glory before the Indians scattered.

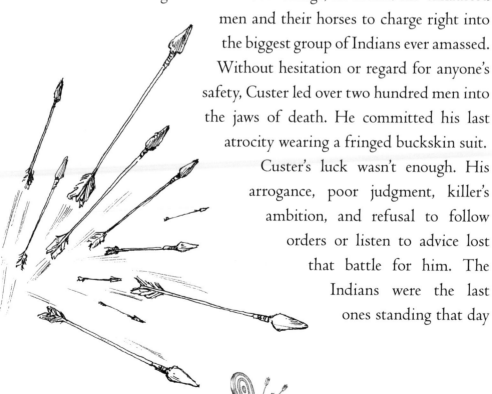

Once Custer got to the Indian village, he forced his exhausted men and their horses to charge right into the biggest group of Indians ever amassed. Without hesitation or regard for anyone's safety, Custer led over two hundred men into the jaws of death. He committed his last atrocity wearing a fringed buckskin suit.

Custer's luck wasn't enough. His arrogance, poor judgment, killer's ambition, and refusal to follow orders or listen to advice lost that battle for him. The Indians were the last ones standing that day because they were actually fighting with conviction, a plan, and a community.

Without flinching, Custer had guided his two brothers, brother-in-law, and nephew to their deaths. His poor sister lost a nephew, three brothers, and a husband.

After Custer died, the Indian women found his corpse and bored a hole in his eardrums because George Armstrong Custer was a man who never listened. Custer didn't heed his military orders or the warnings, and perpetrated a monstrous final act that had Shakespearean proportions.

It's hard to say whether he actually *heard* the line while he watched the forty performances of *Julius Caesar* or not—but it is true, nevertheless:

"The evil that men do lives after them" (III, ii, 84).

A FEW OF CUSTER'S OUTFITS

(Note: Custer was renowned for wearing a bright red tie with many outfits and uniforms.)

- Full-dress major general frock coat, trousers, yellow sash, and tricornered hat
- Sack coat, trousers, wide-brimmed felt hat with stars, gauntlet gloves
- Patterned officer's cloak coat with a curly wool collar and cuffs
- Green corduroy brigadier shell jacket with major general shoulder boards and trousers
- Full Indian-chief buckskins with fringe
- Double-breasted buffalo coat and buffalo-fur pill box hat
- Bib fireman shirt, wide-brimmed silverbelly felt hat (cream colored)

NOT-SO-COOL FACT

In December 1890, the Seventh Cavalry took part in the Wounded Knee massacre. Between one hundred and fifty and three hundred Sioux men, women, and children were slaughtered.

Some of the men from the Seventh Cavalry were veterans of the Battle at Little Bighorn, June 25, 1876.

WARRIORS FROM SITTING BULL'S VILLAGE AT THE BATTLE OF LITTLE BIGHORN

Crazy Horse • Left Hand • Gray Eagle • Comes in Sight • Two Moons
Wolf's Tooth • Yellow Nose • Gall • Wooden Leg • Rain in the Face
Gray Whirlwind • He Dog • Black Bear • Runs the Enemy • Iron Hawk

SAMPLING OF LYRICS IN CUSTER'S THEME SONG

(His Band Played It Whenever He Charged into Battle)

"GARRYOWEN" BY THOMAS MOORE

We are the boys who take delight
in smashing Limerick lamps at night,
and through the street like sportsters fight,
tearing all before us.

We'll beat the bailiffs out of fun,
we'll make the mayor and sheriffs run,
we are the boys no man dare dun,
if he regards a whole skin.

Our hearts so stout have got us fame,
for soon 'tis known from whence we came,
where're we go they dread the name,
of Garryowen in glory.

CHORUS
*Instead of spa we'll drink down ale
and pay the reckoning on the nail,
for debt no man shall go to jail;
from Garryowen in glory.*

THOMAS ALVA EDISON

SHOCK AND AWFUL

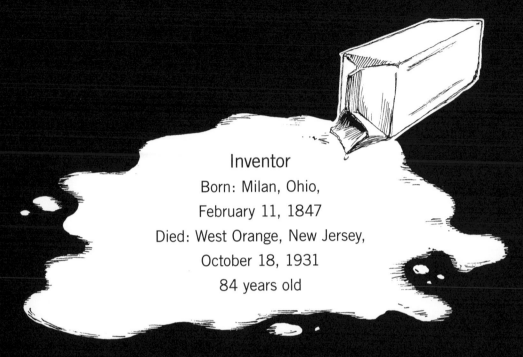

Inventor
Born: Milan, Ohio,
February 11, 1847
Died: West Orange, New Jersey,
October 18, 1931
84 years old

THOMAS ALVA EDISON was a hustling hardworking insomniac who liked the sound of his own name. He cranked out 1,093 patented inventions at a hair-raising clip and slapped his name all over them, even the ones that weren't technically his, and he never looked back (unless he was sued). The problem was, he didn't look forward either. He might have invented the future, but he was a heartless visionary who couldn't see beyond his own nose.

Born in Ohio, Thomas Edison was the youngest of seven children. Everything he touched was a lab experiment, starting with when he wanted to see what would happen after he set fire to the family barn.

What happened was that his dad was so angry he beat Thomas in the town square.

After only three months in school his teacher complained that he didn't pay attention. Since Edison was hard of hearing, it's possible he couldn't hear what they were saying, or maybe he just didn't want to. Either way, Edison dropped out. Little Tom was hardwired to tinker and mess around with poisonous liquids, batteries, and other hazardous stuff—and his mom let him do it in his boy cave in the basement. Since he never learned math, basic physical science, and chemistry, he taught himself by the "oops, that didn't work" method of experimentation, when he'd accidentally melt, explode, or disintegrate something. At only twelve, he got a full-time job selling snacks in the aisles of moving trains. Back then, kids were hired as cheap labor, but Edison was a little wizard at making money. On the

side, he opened a vegetable stand at the station, and he built himself a lab in the train's baggage car until he—oops—set it on fire.

While Edison became a boy entrepreneur, news of the American Civil War came in the dots and dashes of what is known as Morse code to the train stations' telegraph offices. The telegraph was a welcome improvement from the Pony Express, with its horseback riders galloping messages from place to place. Young Edison figured out a way to make money off Morse code by printing up and selling the latest headlines.

It was a dream come true when sixteen-year-old Edison got a job on the night shift at a telegraph office, giving him a playground of electrical doohickeys and wire for him to monkey with while the rest of the world was conked out. For fun, he'd "surprise" other employees by setting up hot wires to electrically shock them while he watched them through a hole. He also rigged a "rat paralyzer" to electrocute rodents and a similar one to snuff out cockroaches. His twisted good time kept getting interrupted when he was fired from four different offices for not doing his job.

Practical jokes aside, Edison thought up hundreds of gadgets for improving telegraphs, like one that printed telegraph messages, and one that could send more than one message at a time. He patented his inventions so when someone used them he'd get paid. He hit the jackpot with $500,000 (worth about twenty times that now) in orders for one of his invented stock-ticker thingies, and he hired one hundred and fifty people to work at his new factory.

The art of small talk or hanging out were not on Edison's to-do list so there was only one way to find a girlfriend—at work. He surprised one of his employees, Mary Stilwell, a girl he had barely spoken to, when he popped the question on the factory floor. Edison was twenty-four and Mary was only sixteen when they got married

on Christmas Day. It was perfect for a workaholic like Edison. He lumped his anniversary in with Christmas and only had to take off one day to celebrate both. After their wedding/Christmas Day ceremony, Edison went right back to work, and the lucky lady got a solid look at what her forever after would be like. The only real sign that he ever went home was that they eventually had three kids. He didn't go home on the days the kids were born either, not even for the son who got his exact name slapped on him, Thomas Alva Edison.

While Edison's wife stayed home alone, he hired a team of like-minded noodlers to invent stuff under his guidance and under his name, "Edison." He boasted to the press that *he'd* have "a minor invention every ten days and a big thing every six months or so."

But at a competitor's lab, Alexander Graham Bell invented something really big—the telephone—and it was the future.

Edison jumped in the game. Being almost deaf, he couldn't hear the voice coming through the phone, so he invented the microphone to make it loud and clear. He crowed that his microphone was hard to invent and that Bell did the easy part. His microphone technology turned into the first phonograph (record player), and the Edison Speaking Phonograph Company was formed. It would be great for dictating business letters, and for teaching elocution. That's the art of using your lungs, tongue, and voice to sound smart. In Edison's mind, playing music was way down on his list of possible uses for his invention. Besides, there was no way he would give musicians money to create music for *his* phonograph, since he disapproved of dance music and he didn't like other kinds of music either. A different "oops" altogether.

At night, when most people were home with their family, Edison was burning the midnight oil working, so he really needed a lightbulb. He needed it so much he exaggerated to the press that he already had one, so that he could raise enough money to work on making himself one. He started the Edison Electric Light Company without a bulb, a lamp, or a clue how to do it. But that didn't stop him. Fifteen months later, Edison (along with sixty of his fellow lab rats) came up with the first glowing lightbulb. As ideas go, it was unbeatable.

He marked his territory with four hundred and twenty-four patents for switches, sockets, and the whole works. And to get electricity to everybody he designed direct current (DC) power plants that were built by his Thomas A. Edison Central Station Construction Department. He knew that if he could turn on lightbulbs all over the place, people would write about *it* and *him* for thousands and thousands of years. He'd be golden. He had to get it right, and for many weeks in a row, Edison never went home. He definitely wasn't lighting up his wife's life. Mary had been ill for years, and sadly she died when she was only twenty-nine years old. Now their three children were without a mother too.

Meanwhile, other inventors, including a guy named Tesla, had a different idea for bringing electricity to people with alternating current (AC). Edison didn't listen to that idea until Tesla sold it to Westinghouse, and people started buying it.

One AC power station could electrify a hundred square miles, not just half a square mile like Edison's DC. That meant rural areas could get electricity too, not just big cities. AC was cheaper and smarter than DC.

Edison got very bossy about anybody improving *his* electricity. But everyone except Edison agreed that his direct-current method wasn't good enough to call it done.

One thing everybody did agree on—electricity was dangerous. With all the new wires hanging in the streets, people were accidentally getting electrocuted. But they still wanted it. And what they wanted was Westinghouse's AC system.

Edison's territory had been invaded and he went to war. At first, because of his reputation, Edison had the public on his side—until he moved into blowhard territory, saying it would be immoral to buy anything electric from anyone who wasn't him. Edison decided to snuff out his competition by proving that Westinghouse's AC system, not his direct current, was accidentally killing people. Edison found a man to advance his cause, Harold Brown. A younger Edison had killed rats and cockroaches, but they were small. He went bigger to prove his point.

Cats were squirmy and had claws, but dogs were easier to work with. The going rate for a donated stray dog to Edison's lab was twenty-five cents.

In the dark of night with the new lightbulbs on, the animal tests were performed with Brown at the helm. After the first night, Edison told Brown to make the experiments more scientific and to take better notes. In the documents of the next night, a fifty-pound half-breed shepherd survived seven electrical shocks and was adopted on the spot by one of the lab assistants so he wouldn't have to suffer anymore. The lucky dog was named Ajax.

Over a two-week period at Edison's lab, forty-four dogs were shocked, killing most of them.

Edison was happy with the conclusions, and he put on a show. The press and eight hundred curious onlookers were invited to watch the next round of animal experiments so that he could win the AC/DC battle in one big flashy presentation. After only one grizzly experiment was completed onstage, a man from the Society for the Prevention of Cruelty to Animals (SPCA) flashed his badge and shut the whole thing down.

But it would take more than that to shut Edison down. He went for broke. Forget dogs, it was time to prove that AC power could kill an animal as large as a man. Still attempting to manipulate the press, Edison invited them back to the privacy of his lab to witness more animal experiments, along with the Medico-Legal Society to make it more official. This time he went for large farm animals (the kind that go "moo," and the kind you can put a saddle on) in the name of science.

Watching the tests gave the Medico-Legal Society the idea to design an electric chair to execute criminals in prison using AC electricity, Edison's competition. It would be a replacement for hangings. Death by AC—mad dogs and criminals. Sweet. Edison was thrilled; his plan had worked better than he imagined. He said that morally he was against the death penalty, but he suggested a term for the electric-chair procedure: being *Westinghoused.*

In the end, despite Edison's inhumane animal testing, the AC system won the war because it was cheaper and easier to install. Edison eventually failed in the electricity business, and today AC powers our world.

Edison made only one public statement about his animal experiments. "I have taken life—not human life—in the belief and full consciousness that the end justified the means." The truth was, both systems were equally dangerous. And Edison knew that all along.

Edison remarried and had three more children. By the end of his life, Edison's name was on hundreds of businesses and inventions. But his son Thomas Alva Edison Jr. attempted to follow in his father's footsteps, and put the Edison name on a few of his own endeavors.

Then daddy Edison took his son to court and put him out of business. After that, Thomas Jr. didn't want anything to do with his dad's famous name. He changed his name to Burton Willard. Talk about a failure.

Edison came up with more inventions you might have heard of, including the movie camera. But once again, as with the phonograph, he didn't see the social value of his invention. He thought it would be an educational tool, and he stubbornly resisted projecting his films on big screens, thinking that watching a movie would be a solitary act.

MOVIE CAMERA

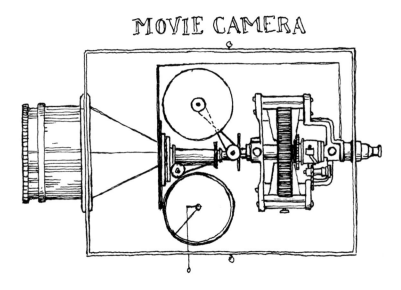

Years before, Edison's top electricians had advised him to abandon his DC system and change to AC. Edison knew they were right, but he was just too stubborn. And he probably could have used a long nap to recharge his batteries. Or maybe he needed all new wiring, the kind that makes you care about other living things.

EDISON'S VISION (OR LACK OF) FOR THE PHONOGRAPH (RECORD PLAYER)

1. Office dictation
2. Reading books aloud
3. Teaching elocution
4. Music
5. Preserving last words of dying people
6. Speaking toys
7. Speaking clocks
8. Language pronunciation
9. Spelling lessons
10. Telephone recorder

CURRENT WARS: AC/DC

DC (direct current) means there is one direction in which the electric current flows. Think of a battery with its + and − sides. The current can start only at one side and end at the other. This is why a battery must face a specific direction. This was Edison's losing current.

AC (alternating current) is capable of reversing its flow of electricity. The current can begin and end at either side: the + or the − source. This allows electricity to travel farther since there are more optional pathways for the current. This current powers your home and everywhere else too.

AS DIFFERENT AS AC/DC

Thomas A. Edison: "I have not failed. I've just found 10,000 ways that won't work."

Nicola Tesla: "If you only knew the magnificence of 3, 6 and 9, then you would have the key to the universe."

EDISON'S 1,093 U.S. PATENTS

(Crossover inventions are listed in both categories)

Electric light and power: 424 • Phonographs and sound recording: 199
Telegraphy and telephony: 186 • Batteries: 147
Mining and ore milling: 53 • Miscellany: 50 • Cement: 49 • Motion pictures: 9

FIRE AND LIGHTNING

- Edison set the family barn on fire.
- Edison started a fire in the baggage car of a train.
- In 1903, the Edison Portland Cement Company's coal-grinding plant exploded, and eight workers were killed.
- In 1914, an explosion in the Film Inspection Building triggered a chemical fire that destroyed more than half of the buildings in Edison's West Orange laboratory. One of Edison's workers and numerous firefighters died. Edison made everyone show up to work the very next day.
- In 1916, an explosion aboard the U.S. Navy's E-2 submarine in the Brooklyn Navy Yard killed five men and injured ten. It is attributed to the hydrogen gas emitted by the Edison batteries installed a few weeks earlier.
- After he had already moved out, in 1914 Edison's home in Menlo Park was destroyed by fire. Then, in 1919 Edison's office and library also went down in fire.
- For the fiftieth anniversary of the lightbulb, in 1929, a tower was built on the location of the original laboratory. A large replica of the Edison lightbulb was on top. It was destroyed by lightning in 1937.
- The dog Ajax, rescued by one of the lab assistants during Edison's animal testing, was killed by lightning.

VINCENT VAN GOGH

LEAST LIKELY
TO SUCCEED

Artist
Born: Zundert,
North Brabant, the Netherlands,
March 30, 1853
Died: Auvers-sur-Oise, France,
July 29, 1890
37 years old

VINCENT VAN GOGH ate paint and drank turpentine. Each swirling, color-loaded brushstroke he painted was a gut-wrenching expression of who he was. His artwork is much loved by everybody, except for all the people who knew him. He couldn't even give away his paintings for free. But Vincent van Gogh kept painting anyway. Anybody in their right mind would have given up. And that's just it; maybe he wasn't. He's famous for never doing a self-portrait with a smile on his face. And why would he? Vincent van Gogh spent a lifetime being harassed and wishing for things he never had: friendship, love, happiness, or an art sale.

Vincent was the oldest of six children. He acted like he was born on a debate team; there was always something to disagree and fight about. Even his grandmother thought he was a pest. His teachers tried beating him into a better mood, and school-yard bullies tormented him, so he was homeschooled, where his volcanic outbursts could only annoy people with the same last name. But after a while, they couldn't take him either. Starting at age eleven, Vincent was sent from one boarding school to the next, each in a different town—his parents hoping he'd reinvent himself as a likable boy someplace else. But he always remained that bothersome and obsessive boy that no one wanted around. Still, he managed to learn three languages and read a lot. Vincent was a brainiac.

By the age of sixteen, Vincent hadn't mellowed any so his minister father passed him off to a wealthy uncle who needed help at the family art gallery. But Vincent's hyperintensity, bad hygiene, and gruff criticism of potential buyers' taste in art had a way of driving away clients. They tried banishing him to a distant stockroom in the London branch where no one could quite understand what he kept yelling about. Unfortunately, the people in London didn't care for that wild look in his eyes either, so Vincent was sent to the Paris gallery.

Maybe they wouldn't dislike him so much if he spoke in French. Wrong. He was unpleasant in all three languages he knew.

Vincent was fired from his own family's art business. But not once in the seven years of being shuffled around within the company did Vincent say, "Hey, I want to be an artist."

That wouldn't come for four more years.

Vincent wasn't a people person. So it was no surprise that he also failed as a bookseller, schoolteacher, and a missionary. Vincent still didn't know what he wanted to be when he grew up. He wandered from town to town, and even though his father sent him money, he chose to wear rags and refused to eat. He was mocked wherever he went.

His family seriously looked into putting Vincent into an insane asylum, but it didn't happen.

Then, out of the blue, when he was twenty-seven years old, and with his usual gusto, Vincent began drawing day and night.

Vincent's family had always encouraged him to draw, and they were thrilled he had a hobby, but what they really wanted was for him to act normal and get a job. His younger brother Theo, who now had Vincent's old job at the art gallery, sent Vincent some money, but eventually Vincent had to move back in with his parents. They were one big unhappy family again.

Vincent would take off into the countryside lugging his pencils, sketch pads, a plank of wood, and a chair. He'd practically force people to pose for him, but mostly they made fun of him, complained he was unpleasant, and thought there was something very wrong with him.

He was scary too, especially when he stalked his own cousin; he kept showing up at her house uninvited. He wanted to marry her even though she hadn't so much as winked in his direction. When

Vincent held his hand over a burning flame, searing his flesh while professing his love for her, he showed his devotion all right—and also that he was very dangerous.

With his museum of bad traits, Vincent hit the road, and the old story played out again and again. Vincent was banished, or escaped, from twenty-five different locations in his short lifetime of thirty-seven years. You do the math.

Brother Theo was resigned to paying all of Vincent's expenses. Vincent promised it would only be temporary until his art sales started pouring in.

Vincent liked working in the blackest black, and he got busy drawing more people. It was sort of like having friends, except he had to pay them. At one point he used Theo's money to buy himself a whole new family: a woman with her newborn baby, daughter, mother, and sister. Vincent offered to pay for their food and their doctor bills, so they all moved in. Plus, they charged him to pose. He had bought the worst kind of relatives. He even bought himself girlfriends, and they repaid him by giving him syphilis.

Vincent's parents were mortified by his behavior, and family relations were at an all-time low when Vincent's dad died suddenly. Vincent's mom blamed the untimely death on Vincent, and she never forgave him.

Theo told Vincent to stop drawing people: Do landscapes. And quit using dark colors. *Paint* something—and use more color! Theo also demanded to see proof of his new colorful landscapes.

Vincent was easy to predict because he would do the opposite of any suggestion. He just used more black, and hunted for more models. The only guy that kept coming back was seventy-two years old and could pose as still as a corpse. It's important to mention he was also deaf.

Out of options, he joined Theo in Paris. Eventually, Vincent started to paint. He boldly signed his paintings—Vincent. But he felt lousy, with toothaches that made his whole head hurt. Sooner or later, one-third of his teeth had to be removed. He hardly slept, he suffered from malnutrition, and he was an alcoholic. But the hardest thing of all was the loneliness. If he wasn't paying, no one ever came to visit. The Parisians called Vincent "truly ugliness personified" and he was banned from painting out in the streets. Even Theo found him unbearable. After a while, the cook quit and no one would pose, so Vincent got himself a really good mirror and painted himself.

Theo was selling paintings by Degas, Monet, and Gauguin while Vincent's work stayed in the closet. To everybody at the time, Vincent's work looked

127

crazy, just like him. They couldn't be separated. No one was buying him or his art.

Two years and two hundred paintings later, Vincent was back on the move, but it wasn't easy. He was weak and suffered from fevers and mouth sores. The local punks in Arles, France, would squeeze out all his paints, and models took advance payments to pose, but then never showed up. Vincent had to paint sunflowers instead. Lucky us.

Theo paid the artist Paul Gauguin to join Vincent in Arles and be his painting buddy. But there was no such thing as someone getting along with Vincent, not to mention their clashing painting methods. While Vincent liked to work outdoors, laying on thick layers of paint 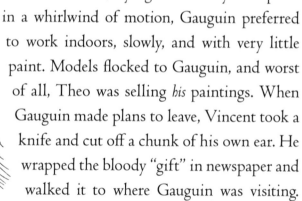 in a whirlwind of motion, Gauguin preferred to work indoors, slowly, and with very little paint. Models flocked to Gauguin, and worst of all, Theo was selling *his* paintings. When Gauguin made plans to leave, Vincent took a knife and cut off a chunk of his own ear. He wrapped the bloody "gift" in newspaper and walked it to where Gauguin was visiting. But the doorman wouldn't let the bleeding artist inside so Vincent handed over the gruesome package and said, "Remember me."

It was impossible to forget.

Gauguin took off with two of Vincent's sunflower paintings and never looked back. During the five months he spent in and out of the hospital for his self-inflicted ear injury, Vincent chased the nurses and jumped into other patients' beds. Sometimes the doctors shackled him to a bed.

Sometime later, Vincent pleaded to go back to his dear friends in Arles. But his so-called friends signed a petition to kick him out of town.

This time his family got their wish: Vincent finally went into an insane asylum.

A retired eye doctor named Dr. Peyron ran the asylum, but luckily it didn't take a brain surgeon to know that painting was good therapy for Vincent. So he was allowed to paint, until he was caught eating his paints and drinking the turpentine. He still came up with an average of one new painting every other day, including *Irises* and *Starry Night*, while he was there.

Theo didn't like *Starry Night*, or any of the hundreds of other paintings that Vincent had been sending to him, saying, "They will undoubtedly be appreciated someday." That was the understatement of the century.

It was decided that Vincent was cured enough to leave the asylum and move to Auvers-sur-Oise near Dr. Gachet, who had treated other artists, like Manet, Renoir, Pissarro, and Cézanne for various ailments.

Vincent lived alone and went out daily to paint. The local teenagers chased him through the streets, put a snake in his paint box, and salted his food. They got him drunk and played other pranks on him.

Two months later, on one of his usual painting excursions, something terrible happened.

129

Vincent came limping back to town with a bullet wound in his stomach.

Guns were rare in rural France. Where did Vincent get one? No one seemed to know.

The police asked Vincent if he had tried to commit suicide. Vincent said, "Yes, I believe so." He also said, "Do not accuse anyone."

Vincent had already cut off his own ear so everybody jumped on the story that now that crazy artist had shot himself—even though the facts didn't add up.

No gun was ever found. All of Vincent's painting gear had disappeared. Vincent was shot in the stomach below the ribs from a weird angle; 98 percent of people trying to kill themselves with a gun aim at their head. And his wound didn't look as if it had been caused by a shot from close range. The bullet was still in his body.

Vincent van Gogh died thirty hours later in Theo's arms on July 29, 1890, in Auvers-sur-Oise, France. He was only thirty-seven years old.

The local church wouldn't hold Vincent's funeral service because he was a suspected suicide. Vincent had to be buried far from the church. Vincent's own mother didn't even come to his funeral, and neither did his four other living siblings. Theo was the only family member there. A few other people who knew him showed up.

Sixteen-year-old René Secrétan was one of the boys who harassed Vincent, and he carried around a .380-caliber gun everywhere he went. It was old and would go off erratically. The day after the shooting, René and his family conveniently left town.

In 1956, when René was eighty-two years old, and Vincent van Gogh's work had become famous, René came forward to tell his account of what happened. He admitted to being the leader of a rowdy group of boys, and that they pestered Vincent for fun. René always had the gun with him, and he claimed that Vincent took it from him and shot himself. But Rene also said he was out of town that day. So which story was true? No one knows for sure.

The shooting was most likely a mean prank that went very bad. Many people knew René owned the gun. But not a single person spoke up. No one wanted to admit that bullying was so wrong. And no one, including Vincent, wanted a teenager to be accused of murder.

Van Gogh saw the world through different eyes than the rest of us, and he was a pill to everyone. And speaking of pills, he could have used some for what some doctors now think he had—a manic-depressive disorder along with temporal-lobe epilepsy. But if he had taken pills to control his mania, he might not have been an artist. A sane Vincent van Gogh might just have been a really good plumber.

It's hard to tell which is more unpredictable, Vincent van Gogh or the art business. Nobody wanted to hang with Vincent back then, but today, *he* won't hang with *you* unless you have about a hundred million dollars to hang a piece of his art on your wall.

He is one of the greatest painters of all time. And for being such an original, Vincent van Gogh got bullied to death at thirty-seven.

"I am myself," he said. That was putting it mildly.

VAN GOGH FAMILY ILLNESS

RECENT THEORIES SUGGEST THAT VINCENT VAN GOGH had temporal-lobe epilepsy and manic-depressive disorder. He wasn't the only van Gogh to suffer from such challenges.

RELATION	PROBLEM
Brother Cornelius	Shot himself and died at thirty-two
Sister Willemina	Spent forty years in an insane asylum
Willem Carbentus (grandfather)	"Mental disease"
Aunt Clara (maternal)	Epileptic
Uncle Hein (paternal)	Epileptic
Uncle Johannes (paternal)	Fits
Uncle Vincent (paternal)	Seizures
Cousin Hendrik (paternal)	Epileptic

THE PAINTINGS NO ONE WANTED

VINCENT SENT THE BULK OF his 900 paintings to his brother Theo. When Theo died only six months after Vincent, his wife, Johanna, was left with a ton of art and a child to feed. She kept the so-called worthless artworks together and occasionally loaned them out to exhibits. Vincent's tragic end played a part in the growing interest in his work, and within two decades he was an established name in the art world. Johanna also published Vincent's letters to Theo in 1914. Her unflinching support for Vincent is credited for getting Vincent van Gogh's work the audience it has today.

ON THE MOVE

VINCENT VAN GOGH MOVED TO A LOT of different towns and cities, crisscrossing the Netherlands, France, England, and Belgium. No one was ever sorry to see him go.

(IN ORDER)

1. Zundert, Netherlands
2. Zevenbergen, Netherlands
3. Tilburg, Netherlands
4. The Hague, Netherlands
5. London, England
6. Paris, France
7. Ramsgate, England
8. Isleworth, England
9. Dordrecht, Netherlands
10. Amsterdam, Netherlands
11. Brussels, Belgium
12. Etten, Netherlands
13. Borinage, Belgium
14. Wasmes, Belgium
15. Cuesmes, Belgium
16. Brussels, Belgium (back again)
17. Etten, Netherlands (a second time)
18. The Hague, Netherlands (a second time)
19. Hoogeveen, Netherlands
20. Nieuw Amsterdam, Netherlands
21. Nuenen, Netherlands
22. Antwerp, Belgium
23. Paris, France (back again)
24. Arles, France
25. Saint Rémy-de-Provence, France
26. Auvers-sur-Oise, France

J. BRUCE ISMAY

FIRST-CLASS COWARD

Ship Owner
Born: Liverpool, England,
December 12, 1862
Died: London, England,
October 17, 1937
74 years old

F J. BRUCE Ismay had had a heart anywhere near as big as his ship, he would have been going someplace. Instead, his life was a series of titanic hit-and-run disasters. Only they weren't all accidents. They were the handiwork of a man with ice in his veins, and the proof is the over fifteen hundred bodies that are at the bottom of the North Atlantic. Bruce Ismay should have gone down with his ship, the *Titanic*, when it sank. Except he slithered into a spot on a lifeboat, claiming that there were no more women and children around to take his seat. That's how things go when you consider everyone but yourself worthless. Look out! Ismay ahead!

J. Bruce Ismay was born in Liverpool, England, in 1862, the second of nine kids. Sibling number one (Bruce's older sister) and sibling number three (younger brother) both died, making Bruce the middle child of two dead ones. The family was getting smaller, but his mother kept at it, cranking out six more, including two sets of twins. It was like Noah's Ark at the Ismay household. Meanwhile, Bruce's father was making his own arks, building and managing a massive fleet of ships called the White Star Line. But no matter how many ships or how many kids the family had, there was no love floating around. The four daughters weren't even allowed to speak during meals or to read the newspaper. Daddy Ismay was a militant brute to everyone, and Mom didn't stand up for her kids. She acted like lack of empathy was a virtue. Mr. Ismay didn't like being in the house at the same time as Bruce. He hated that one day his eldest son, Bruce, would inherit the White Star Line, which his hard work had built from the ground up; his son hadn't had to work for it. Still, he expected that Bruce would follow in his footsteps. Like father, like son.

When Bruce was ten, the White Star liner *Atlantic* sank to the bottom of the ocean. It was the worst nonmilitary sea disaster ever in the North Atlantic. Out of the nine hundred people on board, over five hundred drowned. What few lifeboats there were floated away empty. The story made the front pages of every newspaper in the world in 1873. This was when Bruce fell in love with scrapbooking the history of his family's ships. He cut out every article he could find and glued them into scrapbooks. Even though his feet were still growing, Bruce would follow in his dad's footsteps—drowning people, and he would outdo him by about a thousand people. Bruce couldn't get his coldhearted dad to love him, so he did the next best thing—he became just like him.

At eleven, Bruce was sent to a rich boys' boarding school. Bruce wasn't like the other boys there. Even though Bruce's family had twenty-two servants, they weren't like "real" rich people who inherited their money. The Ismays had worked for their money. There were lots of other ways Bruce didn't fit in as well. The other kids were having fun while Bruce was a brooding loner. His sense of humor entailed sarcastic remarks that bordered on cruel. He was athletic and tall (six foot four) but he never joined a team or made any friends.

After finishing school, Bruce went to work for his dad. Mr. Ismay referred to Bruce as the "new office boy," not as his son. Ismay senior didn't like it that Bruce made every decision as if he had a gun to his head and that he didn't work well with others. It got to the point where Bruce's dad didn't want Bruce around, so he sent him on a slow boat to New Zealand to learn about ships. Nine months later, Bruce Ismay was working in the New York branch of his father's business. Bruce was happy being thirty-three-hundred miles away from his dad; he even fell in love and got married to Florence Schieffelin. Then it was time for Bruce to return to England and become a full-time partner in the business, but he didn't want to work in the same office as his dad. After turning down his dad twice, Bruce finally relented. Ignoring his "stay away from dad" instincts, he headed back to England with his wife and two small children.

On the trip back across the Atlantic, his youngest, six-month-old

Henry, became ill and died soon after they got to London. That was the beginning of the end of Bruce's happiness, even though he and Florence had more kids. When his wife went into labor with their fifth child while on a visit to his mother's house, Bruce's mother kicked Florence out because she didn't want a big mess in her house. The baby was born dead on the horse-and-carriage ride home.

As if things weren't sad enough, their young son Thomas contracted polio and had trouble walking. Bruce despised anyone with a handicap—even his own son. Ismay sometimes made Thomas the brunt of his jokes, but most of the time, he didn't speak to him at all. Ismay decided he didn't like any of his kids and built a separate wing in his house so he wouldn't have to see them or talk to them. Sound familiar? Ismay even bullied his wife, whom he had once loved. When Ismay wasn't working, the only things he liked to do were hunting and scrapbooking newspaper articles about himself and his ships.

After his dad died, Bruce Ismay really wanted to make some headlines of his own. So he planned on building the largest moving man-made objects on the planet. That would be something to scrapbook about! Ismay built *Titanic* and *Olympic*, identical-twin ships.

At this point, trips across the Atlantic Ocean were no longer dreaded. No more weevil-infested hardtack biscuits or sleeping in

bunks eight to a room. Even his *Titanic* third-class accommodations weren't too bad. Although third class *was* on a separate and secured deck of the ship so Ismay and the other rich people wouldn't have to look at the poor people. First class was luxurious, with gourmet food, concerts, and dress-up balls. Ismay's favorite captain, Captain Smith, was nicknamed the "millionaires' captain" because he was so skilled at sucking up to wealthy clients. At forty-nine years old, Ismay was as disliked and alone as he had been at boarding school, and Captain Smith covered for him by hobnobbing with the first-class passengers.

Ismay trusted Captain Smith, which is why he got the honor of taking the helm of the *Olympic*, the ship they sent out many times before its identical twin, *Titanic*. The only reason no one remembers the *Olympic* is because it didn't sink. But it came close, thanks to Captain Smith. Smith crashed it into another ship, cutting an eight-by-fifteen-foot hole in *Olympic*. It had to be towed in. Another time, Smith sailed *Olympic* over a submerged wreck and a propeller blade tore off. Captain Smith was found guilty of recklessness. That should have ended his career, but instead he got a promotion. Ismay wanted Captain Smith for *Titanic's* maiden voyage, violating the unwritten rule of never hiring an officer who had been responsible for a previous disaster at sea.

When Smith brought *Titanic* out of the harbor, he almost crashed it into another ship. Not to mention that they left port while there was a fire burning in one of the vessel's coal bunkers. Maybe . . . just maybe they should have put out the fire before loading up the ship with people. But Smith overlooked that too. *Titanic's* maiden voyage was under way.

The farther *Titanic* got out into the middle of the ocean, the colder it got. On April 14, 1912, it was so cold that most of the passengers stayed bundled up indoors.

Titanic received eighteen ice-related warnings from other ships as it crossed the North Atlantic. Look Out! Icebergs Ahead! The rock-hard hunk of glacier, formed over millions of years, had broken off and floated out to sea. Ismay knew about the ice warnings. It would have been a good time to slow down, but Ismay didn't want that. And Captain Smith couldn't be bothered; he was busy partying with a bunch of millionaires.

So *Titanic* kept plowing forward at 22 knots (25.3 mph), the fastest it had gone on the trip and very close to the ship's maximum speed of 23 to 24 knots.

Every two hours the iceberg spotters up in the crow's nest were switched out so they didn't turn into icebergs themselves.

Despite their best efforts, at 11:40 p.m. on the night of April 14, 1912, *Titanic* hit an iceberg. Ten seconds later, there was a three-hundred-foot gash in the side of the ship.

Ismay felt something—maybe for the first time in his life. He hopped out of bed to find out what it was. He met with Captain Smith; Titanic's designer, Thomas Andrews; and the chief engineer, Joseph Bell. Smith kept the engines going forward for another thirty-five minutes—because how would it look to the press if he had to have another ship towed in? But that made the ship's damaged compartments fill up with seawater even faster. Only Ismay and those other three men knew the ship would be at the bottom of the ocean in a couple of hours. But Ismay knew something else. There weren't enough lifeboats on board because he had decided they were ugly and took up too much space on the rec deck. Thanks to Bruce Ismay's decision there were only enough for 1,100 of the 2,340 passengers and crew on board.

Ismay didn't even bother to warn his valet, who had been working for him for ten years, that the ship was sinking. Or his family's former butler who was now working on the ship. Or his personal attendant on the voyage. Or his secretary. Ismay's heartlessness was titanic.

Ismay's heart told him one thing: get into a lifeboat before they run out of seats.

Captain Smith never gave the order to abandon ship or even to inform the passengers that the ship was sinking. He let all the millionaires keep sipping champagne. Guess they weren't really his friends.

But pretty soon the ship was clearly listing to one side and going down, so the crew started helping people get off without Smith's orders.

Everyone agreed that women and children were to be put in the lifeboats first, but of the 705 people who were saved out of the 2,340 passengers on board, 325 of them were men. And one of them was Bruce Ismay. Ismay knew there were lots of women who didn't have a seat in a lifeboat, and that many of them were locked belowdecks in the third-class area. He later claimed there were no women and children around when he got into the lifeboat. Maybe that is how things looked to a guy who never wanted to help anyone. Ismay wasn't a person who was into saving people or hoisting lifeboats, cutting ropes, or alerting people to danger.

Titanic sank. The lucky ones in the lifeboats watched in horror as it disappeared into the drink.

Everyone but Bruce Ismay. He looked the other way, like it wasn't happening. "I did not wish to see her go down," he said. Ismay also didn't try to save any of the screaming people bobbing in the freezing water even though there was room in his boat.

When the people in the lifeboats were rescued by the *Carpathia*, a ship that had arrived to help the next morning, Ismay got on board and announced, "I'm Ismay, for God's sake get me something to eat.

Get me a stateroom." Meanwhile, the other survivors had to huddle in hallways and comfort each other. Bruce put a sign on the door of his room: PLEASE DO NOT KNOCK.

First order of business for Ismay was to stop paying any surviving crew members since they were no longer *really* working. And he started sending radio messages to the White Star in New York using another name: Yamsi (Ismay backward). He wanted his staff to get him out of New York as soon as he docked because he was getting word that there would be a U.S. Senate hearing on the disaster. And he also knew someplace in that iceberg of a heart that he should *not* have been one of the people who survived. Ismay was going to be a coward once again. He would save himself from public scorn. Others' loved ones were at the bottom of the Atlantic, but Ismay was the real bottom-dweller.

Unfortunately, the U.S. Navy picked up the messages "Yamsi" sent and they were forwarded to the U.S. Senate.

When the *Carpathia* docked in New York there were 30,000 people waiting to see who was still alive. The survivors walked down the gangplank. But not Ismay. He stayed locked in his private room. When Ismay didn't come out, two U.S. senators forced their way into his stateroom and informed him he was to appear the next morning at the Senate's official investigation into the wreck of *Titanic*. There was no lifeboat to save Ismay this time.

At the hearing, Bruce Ismay was asked questions. Do you know what proportion of women and children were saved? Do you know which officers on the ship died? Do you know how many people were in the lifeboats? Are any of the wireless operators still alive? Did the ship break in two?

His answer to all the questions was, "I have no idea. I didn't ask."

Ismay didn't even care enough to ask!

It was the worst shipwreck of all time. It was on the cover of every newspaper in the world—enough to fill a hundred scrapbooks. But Ismay had nothing to say about it.

Bruce got a slap on the wrist and was permitted to go back to England. No one in his family was permitted to mention the disaster or his shameful escape ever again.

Ismay's scrapbooks got pretty thin after that, even though he lived another twenty-five years. But his failure filled many others' scrapbooks instead.

Bruce Ismay's humanity went down long before the ship. He had already shown the people in his family who he really was—now the whole world knew.

WHAT ISMAY WASN'T DOING

ISMAY HID OUT IN A STATEROOM and did *not* inquire about the other survivors, while *Carpathia's* Captain Arthur Rostron issued compassionate orders like these.

- English doctor, with assistants, to remain in first-class dining room.
- Italian doctor, with assistants, to remain in second-class dining room.
- Hungarian doctor, with assistants, to remain in third-class dining room.
- Each doctor to have supplies of restoratives, stimulants, and everything to hand for immediate needs of probable wounded or sick.
- Chief Steward: that all hands would be called and to have coffee, tea, soup, etc., in each saloon, blankets in saloons, at the gangways, and some for the boats.
- To see all rescued cared for and immediate wants attended to.
- My cabin and all officials' cabins to be given up.

BRUCE ISMAY'S ENDGAME

- Ismay retired from the White Star Line a year after the sinking, in June 1913.
- Ismay had made over eighty crossings between America and England. He held the record for the most crossings. But his voyage on the *Titanic* was his last one.
- Ismay was barred from his private club when he got home to England.
- He had loud nightmares that woke up the whole house.
- Ismay's wife banned anyone from mentioning *Titanic* around him.
- He bought a house in a remote area of Ireland so he could hunt and fish alone.

- In a letter to Mrs. Thayer, a woman he met on *Titanic*, he wrote: "*I never liked people and am now worse than ever.*"
- When Ismay went to see a concert, he would go alone, but he always paid for two seats. One for himself and the other for his hat and coat.
- Bruce Ismay had to have his right leg amputated below the knee as a result of his diabetes.
- All four sides of his tomb were engraved with an armada of ships.

TITANIC FACTS

- *Titanic* took two hours and forty minutes to sink after hitting an iceberg.
- A total of 328 bodies were found after the disaster. Of those, 119 were buried at sea.
- On board were 3,500 mailbags containing 200,000 pieces of mail.
- Of the 9 dogs on board *Titanic*, 2 got into lifeboats and were saved.
- Most of the lifeboats on the ship were on the boat deck, for first- and second-class passengers only.
- The binoculars were locked up on the boat and so were not used by the crew to help look for icebergs.
- There were 3,560 life vests: enough for everyone. But the water temperature was only 33 or 34 degrees Fahrenheit, too cold to survive in for more than a couple of minutes.
- Souvenir hunters picked over the lifeboats on the night they arrived. Later, the lifeboats rotted away in a boatbuilder's yard in Brooklyn.
- The main reason *Titanic* sank was human error.

JOSEPH JEFFERSON "SHOELESS JOE" JACKSON

GAME OVER

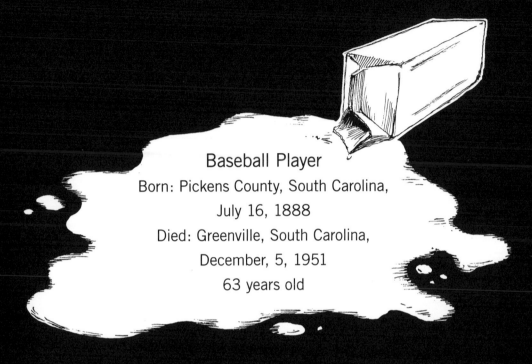

Baseball Player
Born: Pickens County, South Carolina,
July 16, 1888
Died: Greenville, South Carolina,
December, 5, 1951
63 years old

THEY ALL BACKED up when Joe Jackson went to bat. And every pitcher wished he wasn't there. He was a big man who was great at one thing—baseball. His knuckles reached his knees, and his forearms had the circumference of small trees. Joe's supersized limbs could swing a bat and nail a baseball so hard it knocked fielders over—ripped gloves out of their hands. Some ducked to get out of the way. It wasn't just his hitting; he could throw a strawberry through a locomotive. Joe was born knowing how to read the seams on a fastball pitch, but he never learned how to read a word. If he had, he would've read about what happens to cheaters, and maybe Joe Jackson wouldn't have become one and wouldn't have fouled against his own talent.

Joe was the first of eight siblings born in rural South Carolina, in 1888. The Jacksons moved to Brandon village, which was built for one purpose: to house workers for the town cotton mill, who'd marry and have lots of babies who would then grow up and work in the town cotton mill too. Except nobody waited until they grew up to get hired. At about six or seven years old, instead of going to school and learning how to read and write, Joe was inside the mill, sizing, combing, and spooling cotton for seventy hours a week in a haze of cotton fluff. He went home every night with a shirt's worth of cotton in his lungs. If you worked there long enough you'd die from clogged lungs. Most mill workers eventually went deaf from the loud machines. When he was only ten, after a case of measles, Joe's legs became paralyzed for months. He recovered—but then he had to go back to work again, breathing in lint all day.

Mill work was a dead-end poverty trap. The only fun thing for workers to do with their little time off and no money was baseball. You were either playing it or you were in the stands cheering.

Joe's abnormally long arms could hurl a ball farther than a grown man could. So at only thirteen, he got one of the twelve spots on the Brandon Mill team to play against other mill-town teams. Joe Jackson whacked a lot of four-baggers (home runs) and people lined up to watch him do it. Plus, he batted lefty or righty—whatever he felt like—nobody else around was a switch-hitter. As the biggest sensation that ever hit Brandon, he was given an easier job at the mill, and practice time during work hours. He was paid $2.50 per game—

more than he made for a day's work. His life was switching up; he was striking gold.

Baseball fever wasn't just in the mill towns: all of America wanted to see more baseball. There were no professional basketball, football, soccer, or hockey teams. The only other professional sport at the time was boxing. People preferred watching double plays rather than two guys beating the crud out of each other in a boxing ring, so the competition was slim for America's national pastime—baseball was it. Every town had a team, and people loved betting money on who would win. Gambling was America's second favorite pastime; it was baseball, betting, and boxing—in that order.

The whole Jackson clan got in on the gambling too. While Joe played, his five younger brothers would run around in the stands taking bets on whether Joe would get a hit, and then they'd collect the winnings in a hat. Once, they collected $29.75 for a home run: equal to the pay for twenty-five days of work at the mill. Joe playing baseball was a poverty-escape grand slam for his entire family.

Free to follow the money, Joe played on whichever of the thirteen nearby mill teams paid the most. Once, he played a game in his socks because his new spikes had blistered his feet. From then on, his nickname was "Shoeless."

Joe made a smart play when he married Katie Wynn. She had gone to school and could sign the marriage certificate for both of them. They didn't have enough money for a dream honeymoon, but it didn't matter since Joe spent their wedding day playing center field.

Then a real dream came true. In 1908 Joe got on a major-league team, the Philadelphia Athletics. But when it came time for "Shoeless Joe" Jackson to take the six-hundred-mile train trip to Philadelphia, he stayed home.

The Athletics manager sent someone to get him. Except somewhere along the way, Joe hopped off and went back to his family. A second guy fetched Joe, but he had to watch him like a hawk all the way to Philly. No one could believe this "Shoeless" guy wasn't more excited to play in the majors.

Going to the major leagues was a major problem for Joe. Maybe Joe dragging his cleats getting to Philly didn't have anything to do with baseball. The twenty-year-old was a real country boy, and he had never even seen a big city before or been away from his family. Maybe he hesitated because he couldn't read. Joe wouldn't be able to order food from a menu or read a street sign, or deal with about a thousand other things that involved knowing the alphabet. The only thing he could read was a pitch and that made him a major sensation in the majors—when he finally got there.

Joe's bats got proper names like Black Betsy, Dixie, and Big Jim, and his bats even got more press than the other players. Joe was a soft-spoken, mild-mannered lug. His teammates were jealous of his superior ball playing and all the attention his bats got, so they harassed him and called him a stupid yokel. Nasty name-calling was acceptable back then.

It wasn't just in the dugout; it came from the stands too. Fans of the opposing teams yelled, "Can you spell 'cat'?" And you could fill a book with all the newspaper articles about Joe being a dumb hick.

Absolutely no one was winning any good-sportsmanship awards. Top to bottom, baseball teams in the 1910s were full of con men, cheats, and drunks.

Joe ditched the team and went back to South Carolina to be with his people. But the Athletics manager owned Joe's baseball career, so

Joe couldn't play for any other team. It was in the contract that Joe had signed but couldn't read. His career would be over.

No one could figure out what Joe was thinking. The press decided he wasn't thinking at all: "A man who can't read or write simply can't expect to meet the requirements of big league baseball," the sportswriter Hugh Fullerton wrote. Another reporter said: "It was too much for his mental makeup."

Out of options, Joe went back to the team and the mistreatment.

His only answer to the constant bullying was, "I ain't afraid to tell the world that it don't take school stuff to help a fellow play ball." No one ever compared him to Shakespeare. But he was right. It was just a bunch of guys chasing balls and trying to hit it with a stick.

All this abuse made Joe determined to leave the team for good. Who could blame him? The manager could have ended Joe's career right then, but instead of blackballing him he traded him to a team in Cleveland.

Joe stayed in Cleveland, and his family joined him. After a few trades over the years, in 1915 Joe ended up on the Chicago White Sox. He was twenty-eight and holding his own against legendary rival players like Ty Cobb and Babe Ruth.

But then World War I changed everything.

The season was shortened, and attendance dropped by 40 percent. Professional baseball was dying, while corruption within the dwindling game thrived. Teams broke up because eligible players joined the army and average players filled their spots. Joe didn't enlist, and now they called him dumb *and* a coward. But Joe was the sole support for his parents, a few of his siblings and their kids, and his wife. The only uniform they wanted him in was a jersey with a team initial on it.

The White Sox team was far from a smooth operation. The team manager kept most of the money coming in for himself, and didn't pay the players enough. Con men had no trouble finding baseball players willing to lose games on purpose for easy cash.

In 1919, the White Sox made it into the World Series, and they were favored by a long shot to beat the Cincinnati Reds. But something was fishy. It looked like the White Sox were playing to lose—and they did, losing the series five games to three.

The truth came out later. The series had been fixed.

Before the series, a teammate offered Joe $10,000 to help other players on the team lose the series. But Joe said no. Unless Joe was in on the fix it wouldn't work. He wasn't the cleanup hitter for nothing, and a hitting streak could foil the entire scheme. Joe needed to take one for the team or he would blow it for everybody. The second offer to Joe was $20,000. Joe's answer was no. But the fix was still on. Joe asked to be benched, but the coach made Joe take the field.

During the series, Joe was the only player to get a home run, and he had the highest batting average, .375, of all the players on both teams. His twelve hits during the World Series set the record for decades.

After the last game, Lefty Williams, a teammate in on the scam, came to Joe with an envelope full of cash. Joe didn't want it. They argued. Lefty left the envelope with Joe. The next day, Joe attempted to see the manager and tell him what had happened. But the manager wouldn't see him, probably because the manager already knew about the fix, and he'd lose his job if anyone found out.

"Shoeless Joe" Jackson went home with the $5,000 cash, which was an odd amount. Did Lefty think Joe couldn't add either? Joe supposedly hadn't participated, but still, that was *fifteen* big ones short of twenty grand. Maybe their argument had been about how Lefty wasn't coming through with all the money. Or was Lefty just sharing a piece of his own winnings?

There were loads of accusations about a fix. Like all the players on the White Sox, Joe denied it. But a year later, hauled in front of the grand jury investigating the alleged crime, Joe named names and described some of the things he had done to throw the game. But then later, he took back his confession.

No. Yes. No.

Talk about a switch-hitter.

It was hard to know the truth. Strangely, the transcript of Joe's grand-jury testimony retracting his confession disappeared. It turned up five years later in the hands of his manager.

Along with seven other White Sox players, Joe Jackson was thrown out of organized baseball for life, even though they were all acquitted for lack of evidence. But everyone knew the White Sox had

switched to the Lying Sox of baseball. The
White Sox cheating scam became known as
the Black Sox scandal.

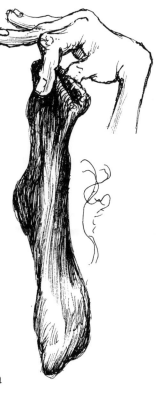

Joe Jackson was a miraculous baseball
player, but it only took two strikes to get Joe
out of baseball: he lied under oath and he took
the $5,000. Whether he cheated or not we
may never know.

"Outlaw" baseball was all Joe was allowed
to play. Back home in South Carolina, Joe ran
a dry-cleaning business, a pool hall, and owned a
liquor store—his long arms weren't swinging any
more bats with names. It was fortunate he never
learned how to read. He didn't need to read over
and over how people thought he was a liar and a
cheat.

Joe was right when he said the lessons you learn in school don't
teach you how to play ball. But he also missed the life lesson that
teaches you how to be true to yourself and what happens when you're
not. Because in the end, he lost more than one World Series; he lost
himself.

"Shoeless Joe" Jackson did what a guy with a gift like his should
never do—he threw it away.

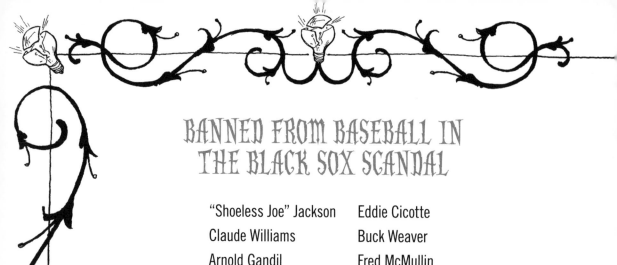

BANNED FROM BASEBALL IN THE BLACK SOX SCANDAL

"Shoeless Joe" Jackson   Eddie Cicotte
Claude Williams   Buck Weaver
Arnold Gandil   Fred McMullin
Charles Risberg   Oscar Felsch

JOE'S BAT "BLACK BETSY"

JOE JACKSON'S FAVORITE BAT STAYED in his extended family for years. In 2001, "Black Betsy" sold for $577,610.00

BASEBALL PLAYERS HAVE GOOD NICKNAMES

Joe Jackson: *Shoeless*   Larry Doyle: *Laughing Larry*
Eddie Collins: *Cocky*   Lena Blackburne: *Slats*
Jim Shaw: *Grunting Jim*   Bennie Meyer: *Earache*
Ray Schalk: *Cracker*   Fritz Mollwitz: *Zip*
Mickey Mantle: *The Commerce Comet*   Carl Hubbell: *The Meal Ticket*

LIVE AND LEARN OR MAYBE NOT

AS A GROWN MAN, JOE was offered one-on-one tutoring to learn his ABCs, but he chose not to. It was another kind of failure for "Shoeless Joe" never to switch from being an illiterate man to a man who could read and write.

DECISION BY JUDGE LANDIS ON THE BLACK SOX SCANDAL

THE IMMUNITY WAIVERS, ORIGINAL CONFESSIONS, and some of the testimony had been stolen from the files. The jury found the eight White Sox players innocent because of the lack of evidence.

Judge Landis's remarks the day after the trial:

"Regardless of the verdict of juries, no player that throws a ball game; no player that undertakes or promises to throw a ball game; no player that sits in a conference with a bunch of crooked players and gamblers where the ways and means of throwing games are planned and discussed and does not promptly tell his club about it, will ever play professional baseball."

HOW TO FIGURE OUT BATTING AVERAGE

FIGURING OUT A BATTING AVERAGE is a division problem. Take the total number of hits and divide it by the number of at-bats. For example: Georgia got 68 hits in 152 times at bat.

$$68 \div 152 = .447$$
Georgia's batting average is .447
Nice!

AMELIA M. EARHART

WINGING IT

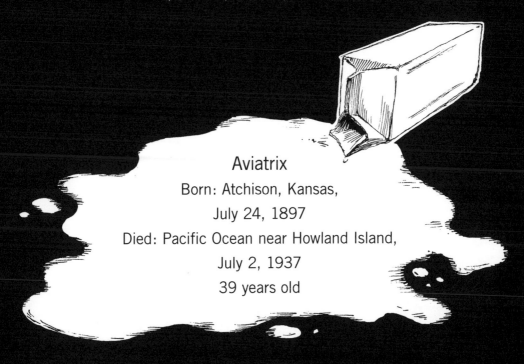

Aviatrix
Born: Atchison, Kansas,
July 24, 1897
Died: Pacific Ocean near Howland Island,
July 2, 1937
39 years old

FLYING AN AIRPLANE in the early 1900s was an extreme sport. A runway was any piece of land without a tree on it, and planes were cramped, loud, blowy places without bathrooms or cup holders. One false move and you'd be dead. It must have been the false moves that got Amelia's heart pumping, not in an "I'm going to die" way, but more in a "That's a blast! I'm doing that again" way. She had what it took for aviation stardom. Besides looking great in piloting outfits, she was fearless, adventurous, and addicted to breaking records. That attitude in high altitude made Amelia Earhart who she was—until the bad odds about gravity caught up with her.

Amelia was born in 1897, in the state of Kansas. It was a world

without airplanes, or even cars, but she was on the move early. At three, when her little sister was born, Amelia went to live with her lonely maternal grandparents to keep them company. Her grandmother could take the fun out of an ice cream sundae, and her grandfather didn't know what day it was. It was a free-for-all over there. Amelia got away with hunting for snakes, sliding off the roof, and going face-first downhill on a sled. She was smart, especially in math. Except she never actually learned the math formulas; she used the same strategy that she used for everything else: she "winged it."

By eleven, Amelia was an independent, freckle-faced beanpole. She moved back in with her parents because her dad got work in another state. Amelia's moody alcoholic dad had to chase down jobs wherever he could. The Earhart family survival strategy was to keep moving, but not always in the same direction. Her parents separated, reunited, and separated again. The Earharts had moved to Kansas, Iowa, Missouri, Illinois, Pennsylvania, Toronto, Massachusetts, New York, and finally California. Amelia wasn't exactly antisocial; she was just unknowable. Mostly because she kept her drunk father on the down low and she was always the new girl in town.

Amelia got around, but her life was going nowhere. The only steady thing she had were chronic sinus infections. At twenty-three,

with a headache, and nothing better to do, she and her impulsive dad went to watch pilots flying airplanes in crazy loops and spins. It was enough to scare anyone, but Amelia signed up for lessons. She zipped herself into a leather bomber jacket and started using "wingspan" in all her sentences. But she was no natural. Amelia crashed planes into hedges, flipped over, careened off runways, stalled out, and forgot to fill the gas tank. Her first instructor told the reckless Amelia to find another teacher. You'd think that would've made Amelia buckle down and be more teachable. But it didn't.

At twenty-four, with inheritance money from her long-gone grandparents, Amelia bought herself an airplane. She probably should have paid for a lot more lessons with that money. Instead, up Amelia went, flying by the seat of her pants, with fearless disregard for the dangers of being that far off the ground. She went so high she set a record, flying higher than any other woman ever had: 14,000 feet. This feat was like driving in the Indy 500 with only your learner's permit. The Aeronautical Hall of Fame put her name on a plaque, and she was in the newspaper. Amelia saw a glimpse of fame—but it didn't last.

The fun she was having wasn't paying the bills. Amelia sold her airplane to pay for a sinus operation. Afterward, she bailed on paying her medical bills and bought a Kissel Speedster Gold Bug car instead. Amelia's parents divorced. Her mother hopped in the car with her and they headed for the East Coast.

At twenty-nine, with no job, no plan, and no real home, Amelia filled out an application at a job-placement agency in Boston. Amelia made up a better version of herself. She lied about going to college. She lied about her work experience. And she lied about her age. Those lies got her hired as a social worker. To raise money for the low-income immigrants she was helping, Amelia hired an airplane and threw fund-raising flyers out the open cockpit. The flyers landed all over town, and Amelia landed in the newspapers again.

But she was just a news blip; the real aeronautic megastar in 1927 was Charles Lindbergh, the first man to fly solo across the Atlantic.

Aviation and Lindbergh grabbed the world's attention. A man named George Putnam was searching for a woman who looked like Lindbergh in a skirt. Someone passed Amelia's name on to George, and he saw the resemblance. Amelia would be the first woman passenger on a flight across the Atlantic.

On the plane, she didn't even get a real seat. She sat in the back with the fuel tanks. But the moment Amelia Earhart's feet hit the ground after the flight, she was a superstar. No one looked twice at the real pilot who flew the plane. The press called Amelia a great pilot, *and* she looked like Charles Lindbergh's sister. People liked looking at her in her man-pants, parachute-fabric shirts, and short boy-cut hairstyle. At thirty years old, in the snap of a finger, Amelia went from a nobody to a person with a book deal, product endorsements, parades in her honor, and a cross-country lecture tour. And she had the pushy PR man George Putnam promoting her every move.

Amelia didn't correct the media's exaggerations about her soaring talents—she embraced them. She purchased a plane and was back in the cockpit. She loved flying but had no interest in fiddling with cool gadgets or even doing the basic maintenance on the plane, like changing the oil. The plane overheated and stalled out. There were forced landings, when she'd demolish landing gears and pretzel the wings. Totaling her propeller was a regular thing. Back at home, George fibbed to the press, blaming Amelia's bang-ups on a phantom updraft or some made-up soggy field.

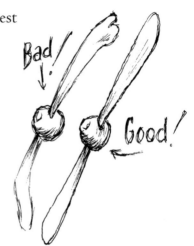

It didn't matter that she had a lot of close calls—she was "winging it" like nobody's business. Clearly, Amelia Earhart had nerves of steel. Maybe up in the sky Amelia found her bliss in the mind-numbing noise while she endlessly played the "what can you see in that cloud" game. Or maybe she went up to get away from everybody down below. Whatever it was, Amelia's willingness to gamble with her life to achieve greatness inspired other women to be brave and to be themselves. But mostly, women wanted to *be* her.

Her publicist, George, wanted to be *with* her. He divorced his wife so he could marry Amelia. She said yes, but only if he agreed never to tell her no about anything. They were a power couple: Amelia had the big name and George was the man behind the curtain.

Unfortunately, her flying prowess didn't grow along with her fame. She continued to overshoot runways, nose over, and bounce into bushes. Once she hit two cars; another time she landed on a fence. Amelia would brush herself off and go break another flying record.

In 1932, Amelia soloed across the Atlantic—refusing to take a

radio or a life raft. Lacking in instrument-panel flying experience, she got lost in a storm and landed two hundred miles off her plotted route. Later, George filmed a staged reenactment of her landing for the press like it was the real thing. It should have been an eye-opener for Amelia, inspiring her to acquire more skills. But instead she did more product endorsements, hung out with world leaders, and was received by the pope.

On her solo flight from Hawaii to California, Amelia took the required radio so she could give her position to the Coast Guard. During the eighteen-hour flight, she reported twice an hour. All she said was, "Everything okay," which was about as helpful as saying, "Whatever."

There was only one more record for Amelia Earhart to set: to be the first person to fly around the equator. Six pilots had flown around the world, but none of those men did it over the thousands of miles of ocean at the equator.

Even Amelia realized it would be a suicide mission to fly this trip alone, so she hired a radio expert, Harry Manning, and a technical adviser, Paul Mantz. Harry and Paul were sticklers for details and preparation. But not Amelia: she pulled some strings so she could skip two out of the three required cockpit-instrument tests: she didn't take the written section or the radio-navigation section. And instead of learning radio navigation, she hired Fred Noonan, an alcoholic navigator, to join her crew.

Thanks to George's marketing genius, the whole world watched as Amelia took off to fly around it. But on the first leg from California to Hawaii, Paul Mantz actually landed the plane when they got there, stealing Amelia's spotlight. George had a hissy fit because the press filmed Amelia *not* flying *her* own plane.

Per George's instructions, Amelia was the only one in the cockpit on the takeoff from Hawaii. Her fellow crew members were crammed in the back as the cameras rolled.

Amelia barreled down the runway as the plane careened right, then left, then right again. The landing gear broke, and the plane belly flopped and skidded 200 degrees around before screeching to a stop. Thankfully, no one got hurt.

Except Amelia and her reputation! She had practically tanked her whole career with this botched takeoff. And George couldn't spin that spinout in Amelia's favor. No matter how hard he tried to blame the crash on a flat tire, the truth was, she'd lost control of the airplane. Strangely, the footage of the non-takeoff/crash has never been found.

A year later, Amelia made a second attempt at the record. Her career couldn't survive another failure, so Amelia snuck off into the sky in the opposite direction. She took only one member of her

What's all this stuff?

original crew, Fred Noonan, the alcoholic navigator. He had recently filed for divorce, sat on his glasses, and been arrested for driving down the wrong side of the street. Even more important, he didn't know Morse code. Neither did Amelia. Morse code was the standard international communication for pilots. Why didn't she take someone who had the skills she lacked? Noonan needed a job, so she hired him. For some unknown reason, Amelia had put a version of her father in the cockpit with her. It was a great gig for Noonan: he'd be taste-testing scotch whiskey around the globe.

Amelia and the pickled navigator made it three-quarters of the way around the globe, but that was flying over continents. The last quarter of the trip was over the Pacific Ocean, and it wouldn't be so easy. They'd take off from Lae, New Guinea, and had to fly across 2,556 miles of ocean to tiny Howland Island. Howland is only 1

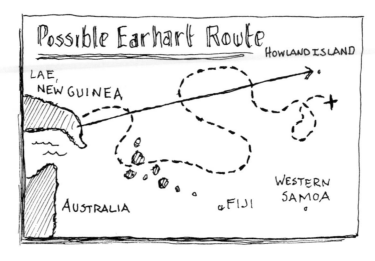

Possible Earhart Route

HOWLAND ISLAND

LAE, NEW GUINEA

AUSTRALIA

FIJI

WESTERN SAMOA

mile wide and 2 miles long. Finding the island would be as hard as spotting a dime on a soccer field from 1,000 feet up while going 180 miles per hour. Just a little cloud cover and Amelia would miss it. But Amelia *needed* to refuel on Howland. Three ships were anchored along the flight route to help Amelia find the island.

George was put in charge of all the radio call times and frequencies. Except he used the year-old and now completely wrong paperwork of her original radio man, with a different flight plan and intending to use Morse code.

George must have known Amelia didn't know Morse code! Amelia had even gone so far as to remove the Morse code sending key and the receiving antenna on her plane. A blunder beyond all blunders. George also knew she had dropped her technical team and that she and Noonan didn't learn how to work the tricky radio equipment. Didn't he? Or was George so used to covering up her shortcomings he couldn't stop?

On top of that, George was hurrying Amelia to finish her world trip by the Fourth of July for an extra publicity boost. It would be a cash cow for them for years. She needed to get her twin-engine Lockheed Electra up, up, and away.

In her rush, Amelia took off from Lae for Howland Island without the latest weather report. Pilots *always* need up-to-the-minute weather data. The headwinds were now 11 miles stronger than what the old report had indicated. That alone drastically changed how much fuel she'd burn and increased her estimated flight time from eighteen hours to nineteen hours. Every weensy thing mattered; every foot of runway, every gallon of gas, every mile of headwind—but this was exactly the kind of stuff Amelia had skipped over her whole life.

Amelia's monumentally stupid decisions were adding up.

On board, Noonan used celestial navigation, the kind of direction-finding technique used way back in Columbus's time. He pointed his gadgets at the sun or at stars to figure out their location. A reasonable margin of error for this course-plotting method is 10 percent. If he calculated their position when the sun came up, they could miss the island by 50 miles.

Seven hours after they took off, radiomen finally heard Amelia give her one and only position report. During the following twelve

hours, they partially heard her report the weather: "Cloudy and overcast" and, "Partly cloudy."

The ship parked at Howland tried signaling her with Morse code and their usual technology to no avail. So they resorted to a caveman solution. They sent up a smoke signal. Except the smoke didn't form a tall column into the sky. It ended up hovering low over the surface of the water, camouflaging the island completely.

Somewhere between Lae and Howland Island, Amelia had reached the point of no return. A pileup of her many missteps equaled disaster, and this time there was no recovery or spin possible. The U.S. Navy searched for her airplane for seventeen days. But Fred Noonan and Amelia Earhart were never heard from again.

It took George a year to finally accept that she was gone.

Amelia Earhart's own failings played the lead part in her death. Risk without knowledge is just "winging it"—a daredevil attitude that will catch up to you sooner or later. Hoping for the best is not a skill. Knowledge is power. And talent is just a starting point for hard work. Blind to her own weaknesses, Amelia cut a few too many corners. And she surrounded herself with people who helped her do so.

Amelia Earhart was a beautiful risk taker, and she went where her talents and the wind blew her. No one in history was ever quite like her.

People have been searching for her since her plane disappeared on July 2, 1937. Every couple of years someone thinks they've spotted her plane on the ocean floor, but nothing has been confirmed yet.

WHAT SHE DIDN'T TAKE

ON AMELIA EARHART'S LAST FLIGHT from Lae, New Guinea, to Howland Island, she decided to remove what she considered nonessential items to allow room for more fuel. That happened to include all the emergency gear.

Flares • Smoke bombs • Spare parts • Extra maps

Books • Tools • Suitcases • Clothing

EARHART'S ROUTE AROUND THE WORLD

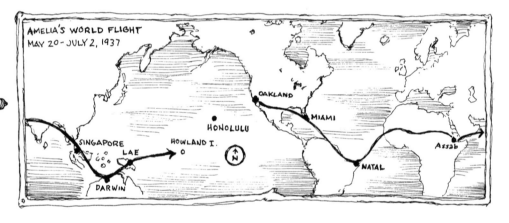

LOCKHEED ELECTRA COCKPIT STATS

AMELIA MOST LIKELY DIED IN HER COCKPIT.

- The two seats were jammed in a space that was 4 feet, 6 inches wide by 4 feet, 6 inches long.
- The cockpit was only 4 feet, 8 inches tall.
- There were no shoulder-harness seat belts.
- There were over 50 dials on the instrument panel.
- It was too loud in the cockpit to hear, so Amelia and Fred had to write messages to each other.

LAST FORTY-FOUR DAYS

MAY 20, 1937~JULY 2, 1937

AMELIA EARHART SPENT THIRTY-FIVE OF the last forty-four days of her life airborne.

SAMPLE FLIGHT TIMES:

Lae to Howland Island . . . . . . 20 hours, 13 minutes
Assab to Karachi . . . . 13 hours, 22 minutes
Natal to Saint Louis . . . . 13 hours, 22 minutes
Paramaribo to Fortaleza . . . . . . 9 hours, 20 minutes
Tucson to New Orleans. . . . . . . 8 hours, 40 minutes

NOT-SO-COOL FACT

AMELIA EARHART CRASHED TWICE TRYING to fly to Howland Island. The first time, she crashed while taking off from Hawaii heading to Howland. The second time, leaving Lae from the opposite direction, she crashed into the Pacific Ocean somewhere near Howland. It wasn't meant to be.

AMELIA'S DISTINCTIVE LOOK

- She wore pants because she didn't like her ankles.
- Amelia's short hair had a carefree just-woke-up look, but Amelia curled it every day.
- She never smiled with her mouth open because she had a large gap between her front teeth.

ONE MORE THING

THERE ARE SO many ways to fail that it's hard to pick which one is right for you. The possibilities are limitless, and the world is your failure playground. You can fail in ways you won't even be able to predict. You'll dive into things you'll never finish, and finish stuff that stinks. Sometimes you'll try really hard, and that won't be enough.

Some people have good intentions, but end up failing anyway, like Susan B. Anthony and Vincent van Gogh. But that's not true for everyone. No one can ever say that except for the spying, cheating, and looting, Benedict Arnold was a really great guy. There's no way to put a good spin on a failure like that. It's over. So don't do that.

There's no way to succeed at failing either. So fail the best you can: try something new, be brave, make mistakes. Just don't hurt anyone, don't get greedy, and don't act like you're perfect, because you're not.

Good luck, and good-bye.

ACKNOWLEDGMENTS

FIRST, MY THANKS TO Edward Necarsulmer IV, who believed in me way before I believed in myself. And to Emily Easton for her support and guidance.

A very special thanks to Leah Komaiko for helping me say what I really mean to say, and to Angela Wiencek-Ashe, a librarian making a difference. Thanks to Cathleen Young for her surgical edits and storytelling wisdom.

I bow to my writers' group: Victoria Beck, Christine Bernardi, Tracy Holczer, Leslie Margolis, Rebecca Mohan, Elizabeth Passarelli, and Anne Reinhard. I can't write books without them. Thanks to my dad, Charles Bragg, for letting me steal his jokes, and my brother, Chick Bragg, for his clear perceptions when I was stuck.

I thank, as always, Maisy Bragg and Cody Rosenfield. They are why I write books in the first place. And then there's Harvey Rosenfield—why speak.

These have been a difficult couple of years. I faced the publication of my previous book, *How They Croaked*, with bloodshot eyes, worried nights, and medical appointments. My mother, Jennie Bragg, was dying of cancer as that book about death hit the bookstores. I'd like to thank all the kind people who helped me during that time. My mom didn't even finish high school, but she was one of the smartest people I've ever known. This book was hard to write without her.

SOURCES

MARCO POLO

Bergreen, Laurence. *Marco Polo: From Venice to Xanadu.* New York: Vintage Books, 2007.

Bettex, Albert. *The Discovery of the World.* New York: Simon and Schuster, 1960.

Larner, John. *Marco Polo and the Discovery of the World.* New Haven, CT: Yale University Press, 1999.

Lester, Toby. *The Fourth Part of the World: The Race to the Ends of the Earth, and the Epic Story of the Map That Gave America Its Name.* New York: Free Press, 2009.

Marsden, William, ed. *The Travels of Marco Polo: The Venetian.* Garden City, NY: Garden City Books, 1948.

Olschki, Leonardo. *Marco Polo's Asia: An Introduction to His "Description of the World" Called "Il Milione."* Berkeley, CA: University of California Press, 1960.

ISABELLA OF CASTILE

Anderson, James M. *Daily Life During the Spanish Inquisition.* Westport, CT: Greenwood Press, 2002.

Carroll, Warren H. *Isabel of Spain: The Catholic Queen.* Front Royal, VA: Christendom Press, 1991.

Edwards, John. *Ferdinand and Isabella* (Profiles in Power). Harlow, England: Pearson, 2005.

Kamen, Henry. *The Spanish Inquisition: A Historical Revision.* New Haven, CT: Yale University Press, 1997.

Mariejol, Jean Hippolyte. *The Spain of Ferdinand and Isabella*. Trans. Benjamin Keen. New Brunswick, NJ: Rutgers University Press, 1961.

Murphy, Cullen. *God's Jury: The Inquisition and the Making of the Modern World*. Boston: Houghton Mifflin Harcourt, 2012.

Rubin, Nancy. *Isabella of Castile: the First Renaissance Queen*. New York: ASJA Press, 1991.

MONTEZUMA II

Brown, Dale M., ed. *Aztecs: Reign of Blood & Splendor*. Alexandria: Time-Life Books, 1992.

Levy, Buddy. *Conquistador: Hernan Cortes, King Montezuma, and the Last Stand of the Aztecs*. New York: Bantam Books, 2008.

Prescott, William H. *History of the Conquest of Mexico*. New York: The Modern Library, 2001.

Thomas, Hugh. *Conquest: Montezuma, Cortes, and the Fall of Old Mexico*. New York: Simon & Schuster Paperbacks, 1993.

FERDINAND MAGELLAN

Bergreen, Laurence. *Over the Edge of the World: Magellan's Terrifying Circumnavigation of the Globe*. New York: William Morrow, 2003.

Daniel, Hawthorne. *Ferdinand Magellan*. New York: Doubleday & Company, 1964.

Morison, Samuel Eliot. *The European Discovery of America: Volume 2, The Southern Voyages A.D. 1492–1616*. New York: Oxford University Press, 1974.

Parry, J. H. *The Discovery of the Sea*. New York: Dial Press, 1974.

Pigafetta, Antonio. *Magellan's Voyage: A Narrative Account of the First Circumnavigation*. Mineola, NY: Dover Publications, 1994.

Roditi, Edouard. *Magellan of the Pacific*. New York: McGraw-Hill Book Company, 1972.

Zweig, Stefan. *Conqueror of the Seas: The Story of Magellan*. New York: Viking Press, 1938.

SOURCES

Online Sources:

"Age of Exploration." *History of Geography.* About.com, 2012.
  http://geography.about.com/od/historyofgeography/a/ageexploration.htm

"Famous Explorers." *Elizabethan Era,* 2008.
  http://www.elizabethan-era.org.uk/famous-explorers.htm

"List of Straits." *Wikipedia,* May 2012.
  http://en.wikipedia.org/wiki/List_of_straits

"Strait." *National Geographic Online.* National Geographic, 2012.
  http://education.nationalgeographic.com/education/encyclopedia/
  strait/?ar_a=1&ar_r=3

"Strait of Magellan." *New World Encyclopedia Online.* New World Encyclopedia, 2009.
  http://www.newworldencyclopedia.org/entry/Strait_of_Magellan

ANNE BOLEYN

Bernard, G. W. *Anne Boleyn: Fatal Attractions.* New Haven: Yale University Press, 2010.

Ives, Eric. *The Life and Death of Anne Boleyn.* Malden, MA: Blackwell Publishing, 2004.

Wallace, William E. *Michelangelo: The Artist, the Man, and His Times.* New York: Cambridge University Press, 2010.

Warnicke, Retha M. *The Rise and Fall of Anne Boleyn: Family Politics at the Court of Henry VIII.* Cambridge, UK: Cambridge University Press, 1989.

Weir, Alison. *The Lady in the Tower: The Fall of Anne Boleyn.* New York: Ballantine Books, 2010.

Weir, Alison. *The Six Wives of Henry VIII.* New York: Grove Press, 1991.

ISAAC NEWTON

Ackroyd, Peter. *Newton.* New York: Nan A. Talese, 2006.

Berlinski, David. *Newton's Gift: How Sir Isaac Newton Unlocked the System of the World.* New York: The Free Press, 2000.

Emsley, John. *The Elements of Murder: A History of Poison*. New York: Oxford University Press, 2005.

Gleick, James. *Isaac Newton*. New York: Pantheon Books, 2003.

Hall, A. Rupert. *Isaac Newton: Adventurer in Thought*. Oxford: Blackwell Publishers, 1992.

Levenson, Thomas. *Newton and the Counterfeiter: The Unknown Detective Career of the World's Greatest Scientist*. Boston: Houghton Mifflin Harcourt, 2009.

Osserman, Robert. *Poetry of the Universe*. New York: Anchor Books, 1996.

Westfall, Richard S. *The Life of Isaac Newton*. Cambridge, UK: Cambridge University Press, 1993.

BENEDICT ARNOLD

Axelrod, Alan. *The Real History of the American Revolution: A New Look at the Past*. New York: Sterling Publishing, 2007.

Boylan, Brian Richard. *Benedict Arnold, The Dark Eagle*. New York: W. W. Norton & Company, 1973.

Flexner, James Thomas. *The Traitor and the Spy: Benedict Arnold and John Andre*. New York: Harcourt, Brace and Company, 1953.

Jacob, Mark and Stephen H. Case. *Treacherous Beauty: Peggy Shippen, the Woman Behind Benedict Arnold's Plot to Betray America*. Guilford, CT: Lyons Press, 2012.

Martin, James Kirby. *Benedict Arnold, Revolutionary Hero: An American Warrior Reconsidered*. New York: New York University Press, 1997.

Randall, Willard Sterne. *Benedict Arnold: Patriot and Traitor*. New York: Quill, 1990.

SUSAN B. ANTHONY

Barry, Kathleen. *Susan B. Anthony: A Biography of a Singular Feminist*. New York: New York University Press, 1988.

Dandelion, Pink. *The Quakers: A Very Short Introduction*. Oxford: Oxford University Press, 2008.

Hudson, Valerie M., et al. *Sex and World Peace*. New York: Columbia University Press, 2012.

Hull, N. E. H., ed. *The Woman Who Dared to Vote: The Trial of Susan B. Anthony*. Lawrence: University Press of Kansas, 2012.

Lichter, Ida. *Muslim Women Reformers: Inspiring Voices Against Oppression*. Amherst: Prometheus Books, 2009.

Robertson, Nan. *The Girls in the Balcony: Women, Men, and* The New York Times. New York: Random House, 1992.

Ward, Geoffrey C. *Not For Ourselves Alone: The Story of Elizabeth Cady Stanton and Susan B. Anthony, an Illustrated History*. New York: Alfred A. Knopf, 1999.

Worden, Minky, ed. *The Unfinished Revolution: Voices from the Global Fight for Women's Rights*. New York: Seven Stories Press, 2012.

Online Sources:

"Human Rights Facts & Figures." *Women's Learning Partnership For Rights, Development, and Peace*. Women's Learning Partnership (WLP), January 23, 2006. www.learningpartnership.org/lib/human-rights-facts-figures

"Poverty is a Human Rights Issue." *Human Rights Now Blog*. Amnesty International, October 17, 2011. blog.amnestyusa.org/escr/poverty-is-a-human-rights-issue/

"Women's History Month: March 2013." *U.S. Census Bureau News*. United States Census Bureau, February 7, 2013. www.census.gov/newsroom/releases/archives/facts_for_features_special_editions/cb13-ff04.html

GEORGE ARMSTRONG CUSTER

Custer, General George Armstrong. *My Life on the Plains Or, Personal Experiences With Indians*. Norman: University of Oklahoma Press, 1962.

Donovan, James. *A Terrible Glory: Custer and the Little Bighorn—the Last Great Battle of the American West*. New York: Back Bay Books, 2008.

Elliott, Michael A. *Custerology: The Enduring Legacy of the Indian Wars and George Armstrong Custer*. Chicago: University of Chicago Press, 2007.

Hammer, Kenneth, ed. *Custer in '76: Walter Camp's Notes on the Custer Fight.* Provo, UT: Brigham Young University Press, 1976.

Koster, John. *Custer Survivor: The End of a Myth, the Beginning of a Legend.* Palisades, NY: Chronology Books, 2010.

McMurtry, Larry. *Custer.* New York: Simon & Schuster, 2012.

Overfield II, Loyd J., ed. *The Little Big Horn 1876: The Official Communications, Documents and Reports With Rosters of the Officers and Troops of the Campaign.* Glendale: Arthur H. Clark Company, 1971.

Oxford Dictionary of Quotations. 3rd ed. New York: Oxford University Press, 1979.

Philbrick, Nathaniel. *The Last Stand: Custer, Sitting Bull, and the Battle of Little Bighorn.* New York: Viking, 2010.

THOMAS ALVA EDISON

Adkins, Jan. *Thomas Edison.* New York: DK Publications, 2009.

Conot, Robert. *A Streak of Luck.* New York: Seaview Books, 1979.

Delano, Marfe Ferguson. *Inventing the Future: A Photobiography of Thomas Alva Edison.* Washington, DC: National Geographic Society, 2002.

Israel, Paul. *Edison: A Life of Invention.* New York: John Wiley & Sons, 1998.

Josephson, Matthew. *Edison.* New York: McGraw-Hill Book Company, 1959.

McNichol, Tom. *AC/DC: The Savage Tale of the First Standards War.* San Francisco: Jossey-Bass, 2006.

Stross, Randall E. *The Wizard of Menlo Park: How Thomas Alva Edison Invented the Modern World.* New York: Three Rivers Press, 2007.

Wearing, Judy. *Edison's Concrete Piano: Flying Tanks, Six-Nippled Sheep, Walk-On-Water Shoes and 12 Other Flops From Great Inventors.* Toronto: ECW Press, 2009.

Woodside, Martin. *Thomas A. Edison: The Man Who Lit Up the World.* New York: Sterling, 2007.

SOURCES

Online Sources:

"Edison Sees His Vast Plant Burn." *The New York Times*, December 10, 1914. http://query.nytimes.com/gst/abstract.html?res=F40614FF3F5C13738 DDDA90994DA415B848DFID3

VINCENT VAN GOGH

Bassil, Andrea. *Vincent van Gogh*. The Lives of the Artists. Milwaukee, WI: World Almanac Library, 2004.

Dorn, Roland, et al. *Van Gogh Face to Face: The Portraits*. New York: Thames & Hudson, 2000.

Gayford, Martin. *The Yellow House: Van Gogh, Gauguin, and Nine Turbulent Weeks in Provence*. Boston: Houghton Mifflin Company, 2006.

Kendall, Richard. *Van Gogh's Van Goghs: Masterpieces from the Van Gogh Museum, Amsterdam*. Washington: National Gallery of Art, 1998.

Naifeh, Steven and Gregory White Smith. *Van Gogh: The Life*. New York: Random House, 2011.

Plazy, Gilles. *In the Footsteps of Van Gogh*. New York: Penguin Studio Books, 1998.

Saltzman, Cynthia. *Portrait of Dr. Gachet: The Story of a Van Gogh Masterpiece*. New York: Viking Penguin, 1998.

Van Gogh, Vincent. *Vincent van Gogh: The Drawings*. New York: Metropolitan Museum of Art, and Amsterdam: Van Gogh Museum, 2005.

J. BRUCE ISMAY

Bartlett, W. B. *Why the Titanic Sank*. Gloucestershire, UK: Amberley Publishing, 2012.

Butler, Daniel Allen. *Unsinkable: The Full Story of RMS Titanic*. Mechanicsburg, PA: Stackpole Books, 1998.

Davenport-Hines, Richard. *Voyagers of the Titanic: Passengers, Sailors, Shipbuilders, Aristocrats, and the Worlds They Came From*. New York: William Morrow, 2012.

Davie, Michael. *Titanic: The Death and Life of a Legend*. New York: Vintage Books, 2012.

Eaton, John P. and Charles A. Hass. *Titanic: Triumph and Tragedy*. 2nd ed. New York: W. W. Norton & Company, 1995.

Everett, Marshall, ed. *Wreck and Sinking of the Titanic: The Ocean's Greatest Disaster*. New York: Harper Design, 2011.

Green, Rod. *Building the Titanic: An Epic Tale of the Creation of History's Most Famous Ocean Liner*. Pleasantville, NY: Reader's Digest Association, 2005.

Maxtone-Graham, John. *Titanic Tragedy: A New Look at the Lost Liner*. New York: W. W. Norton & Company, 2011.

Wilson, Frances. *How to Survive the Titanic: The Sinking of J. Bruce Ismay*. New York: Harper Perennial, 2012.

JOSEPH JEFFERSON "SHOELESS JOE" JACKSON

Bondy, Filip. *Who's on Worst?: The Lousiest Players, Biggest Cheaters, Saddest Goats and Other Antiheroes in Baseball History*. New York: Doubleday, 2013.

Fleitz, David L. *Shoeless: The Life and Times of Joe Jackson*. Jefferson: McFarland & Company, 2001.

Gropman, Donald. *Say It Ain't So, Joe!: The True Story of Shoeless Joe Jackson*. New York: Citadel Press, 1979.

James, Bill. *The New Bill James Historical Baseball Abstract*. New York: Free Press, 2001.

AMELIA M. EARHART

Backus, Jean L. *Letters from Amelia, 1901–1937*. Boston: Beacon Press Books, 1982.

Brennan, T. C. Buddy. *Witness to the Execution: The Odyssey of Amelia Earhart*. Frederick, CO: Renaissance House Publishers, 1988.

Butler, Susan. *East to the Dawn: The Life of Amelia Earhart*. Cambridge, MA: Da Capo Press, 1999.

SOURCES

Long, Elgen M. and Marie K. Long. *Amelia Earhart: The Mystery Solved*. New York: Simon & Schuster, 1999.

Lovell, Mary S. *The Sound of Wings: The Life of Amelia Earhart*. New York: St. Martin's Press, 1989.

Rich, Doris L. *Amelia Earhart: A Biography*. Washington, DC: Smithsonian Institution Press, 1989.

Russo, Carolyn. *Women and Flight: Portraits of Contemporary Women Pilots*. Washington, DC: The National Air and Space Museum, Smithsonian Institution, 1997.

Wels, Susan. *Amelia Earhart: The Thrill of It*. Philadelphia: Running Press Book Publishers, 2009.

Winters, Kathleen C. *Amelia Earhart: The Turbulent Life of an American Icon*. New York: Palgrave Macmillan, 2010.

FURTHER READING AND SURFING

MARCO POLO

Holub, Joan. *Who Was Marco Polo?* Illustrated by John O'Brien and Nancy Harrison. New York: Grosset & Dunlap, 2007.

Morley, Jacqueline. *You Wouldn't Want to Explore with Marco Polo!: A Really Long Trip You'd Rather Not Take.* Illustrated by David Antram. Danbury, CT: Franklin Watts, 2010.

Twist, Clint. *Marco Polo: History's Great Adventurer* (Historical Notebooks). Somerville, MA: Candlewick, 2011.

http://www.history.com/videos/marco-polo#marco-polo
   This site features a goofy yet factual song about the life of Marco Polo.

http://sluggosghoststories.blogspot.com/2012/04/ghost-of-marco-polos-wife.html
   Maybe Marco Polo married Kublai Khan's daughter Hao Dong. Maybe he was imprisoned for marrying her. Maybe she set herself on fire, flung herself out a window, and drowned in the Venice canals out of despair. Maybe her ghost still haunts those canals. Maybe none of this is true.

http://www.gohistorygo.com/#!marco-polo/c1kix
   An informative, easy-to-read history of Marco Polo with video and map links.

ISABELLA OF CASTILE

Bridges, Shirin Yim. *Isabella of Castile* (The Thinking Girl's Treasury of Real Princesses). Illustrated by Albert Nguyen. Foster City, CA: Goosebottom Books, 2010.

Krull, Kathleen. *Lives of Extraordinary Women: Rulers, Rebels (and What the Neighbors Thought)*. Illustrated by Kathryn Hewitt. Boston: HMH Books for Young Readers, 2000.

Meyer, Carolyn. *Isabel: Jewel of Castilla, Spain 1466* (The Royal Diaries). New York: Scholastic, 2000.

http://www.pcgs.com/books/commemoratives/Chapter08-008.aspx
The board of lady managers for the World's Columbian Exposition was formed in Chicago in 1893 at the insistence of Susan B. Anthony. They decided to sell a coin at the exposition to honor Queen Isabella, who famously backed Columbus's voyage. She was the first woman to be featured on a commemorative coin.

http://www.usmint.gov/kids/
This site teaches more facts about the Isabella coin as well as any other U.S. coin you may wish to find.

MONTEZUMA II

DK. *Aztec, Inca & Maya* (DK Eyewitness Books). New York: DK Publishing, 2011.

Kimmel, Eric A. *Montezuma and the Fall of the Aztecs*. Illustrated by Daniel San Souci. New York: Holiday House, 2000.

http://www.nps.gov/moca/index.htm
Montezuma did not fail at getting a national park named after him. Of course, he had nothing to do with the castle and died well before his name was ever attached to it.

FERDINAND MAGELLAN

Bailey, Katharine. *Ferdinand Magellan: Circumnavigating the World* (In the Footsteps of Explorers). New York: Crabtree Publishing Company, 2005.

Kramer, Sydelle. *Who Was Ferdinand Magellan?* Illustrated by Elizabeth Wolf and Nancy Harrison. New York: Grosset & Dunlap, 2004.

Waldman, Stuart. *Magellan's World* (Great Explorers). Illustrated by Gregory Manchess. New York: Mikaya Press, 2007.

http://ageofex.marinersmuseum.org/
> This offers an extensive look at all the world explorers, including Magellan. You can click on any explorer to be linked to further info about that explorer's journey. You'll also learn who was beheaded and who was cannibalized.

http://www.elizabethan-era.org.uk/ferdinand-magellan.htm
> This website has, quite possibly, all you'll ever need to know about Magellan, told in short bullet points—no paragraphs getting in the way here.

ANNE BOLEYN

Meyer, Carolyn. *Doomed Queen Anne* (A Young Royals Book). Boston: HMH Books for Young Readers, 2004.

Price, Sean Stewart. *Henry VIII: Royal Beheader* (A Wicked History). New York: Scholastic, 2009

http://tudorhistory.org
> This website will tell you all you ever wanted and didn't want to know about the Tudors.

http://www.nationalarchives.gov.uk/henryviii/
> There is some fun information here about the rules people in court had to follow, like who is allowed to touch the king and who isn't.

ISAAC NEWTON

Graham, Ian. *You Wouldn't Want to Be Sir Isaac Newton!* Illustrated by David Antram. Danbury, CT: Franklin Watts, 2013.

Hollihan, Kerrie Logan. *Isaac Newton and Physics for Kids: His Life and Ideas with 21 Activities* (For Kids series). Chicago: Chicago Review Press, 2009.

Krull, Kathleen. *Isaac Newton* (Giants of Science). Illustrated by Boris Kulikov. New York: Puffin, 2008.

BENEDICT ARNOLD

Burgan, Michael. *Benedict Arnold: American Hero and Traitor* (Graphic Biographies). Illustrated by Terry Beatty. Minneapolis, MN: Capstone Press, 2007.

Gunderson, Jessica. *Benedict Arnold: Battlefield Hero or Selfish Traitor?* (Fact Finders). Minneapolis, MN: Capstone Press, 2013.

Sheinkin, Steve. *The Notorious Benedict Arnold: A True Story of Adventure, Heroism & Treachery*. New York: Square Fish Books, 2013.

SUSAN B. ANTHONY

Colman, Penny. *Elizabeth Cady Stanton and Susan B. Anthony: A Friendship That Changed the World*. New York: Henry Holt and Co., 2011.

Wallner, Alexandra. *Susan B. Anthony*. New York: Holiday House, 2012.

Weidt, Maryann N. *Fighting for Equal Rights: A Story about Susan B. Anthony* (A Creative Minds Biography). Illustrated by Amanda Sartor. Minneapolis, MN: Lerner Publishing Group, 2004.

GEORGE ARMSTRONG CUSTER

Goble, Paul. *Custer's Last Battle: Red Hawk's Account of the Battle of the Little Bighorn*. Bloomington, IN: Wisdom Tales Press, 2013.

Link, Theodore. *George Armstrong Custer: General of the U.S. Cavalry* (Primary Sources of Famous People in American History). New York: Rosen Publishing, 2004.

http://amhistory.si.edu/militaryhistory/
The Smithsonian National Museum of American History's exhibit *The Price of Freedom: Americans At War* features stories and relics of the many wars America has fought. You can find Custer's famous jacket on display here along with weapons he could have fought with and against.

THOMAS ALVA EDISON

Adkins, Jan. *DK Biography: Thomas Edison*. New York: DK Publishing, 2009.

Barretta, Gene. *Timeless Thomas: How Thomas Edison Changed Our Lives*. New York: Henry Holt and Co., 2012.

Frith, Margaret. *Who Was Thomas Alva Edison?* Illustrated by John O'Brien and Nancy Harrison. New York: Grosset & Dunlap, 2005.

Venezia, Mike. *Thomas Edison: Inventor with a Lot of Bright Ideas* (Getting to Know the World's Greatest Inventors & Scientists). Chicago: Children's Press, 2009.

http://www.time.com/time/specials/packages/article/0,28804,1910417_1910419_1910460,00.html
Edison is famous for saying, "Genius is about 2 percent inspiration and 98 percent perspiration." That is, of course, true when you've paid for, borrowed, or flat-out stolen many of your inventions.

http://www.thehenryford.org/exhibits/pic/2004/july.asp#more
The Henry Ford Museum has a test tube that may contain Edison's last breath. One story states Edison's son captured the breath on behalf of Ford. The other story is that the test tube was just sitting in his room at the time of his death.

http://www.pbs.org/wgbh/amex/edison/sfeature/acdc.html
"War of Currents"
The above link has a great interactive illustration of DC and AC. Also, it is part of a program called "Edison's Miracle of Light."

http://www.biography.com/people/thomas-edison-9284349?page=3
As a friend of Henry Ford, one of Edison's missions was to build a battery for an electric-powered car. Thank goodness he got that invention off the ground so we don't have to rely on gasoline. Oh wait . . . that didn't . . . hmmmm . . . never mind.

http://blog.modernmechanix.com/edisons-own-secret-spirit-experiments/
Edison was a ghostbuster wannabe
Edison firmly believed in ghosts. He made a device, using electricity, that would react if any ghost crossed its path, and he hired a bunch of spiritualists to summon the dead. For thirteen years, Edison kept the results of this experiment secret. Why? Because it was a complete failure. That's why.

VINCENT VAN GOGH

Bernard, Bruce. *Van Gogh: Explore Vincent van Gogh's Life and Art, and the Influences That Shaped His Work* (DK Eyewitness Books). New York: DK Publishing, 2000.

Greenburg, Jan and Sandra Jordan. *Vincent van Gogh: Portrait of an Artist*. New York: Dell Yearling, 2003.

Sabbeth, Carol. *Van Gogh and the Post-Impressionists for Kids: Their Lives and Ideas, 21 Activities* (For Kids series). Chicago: Chicago Review Press, 2011.

http://www.vangoghgallery.com/
This website offers you the chance to view all of van Gogh's works. There is even a list of all the stolen paintings.

http://www.metmuseum.org/toah/hd/gogh/hd_gogh.htm
This link leads you to the Vincent van Gogh page on the Metropolitan Museum of Art website. It features an extremely informative biography and suggestions for further reading. Or, go to the Metropolitan Museum and see for yourself!

http://www.pbs.org/wgbh/nova/sciencenow/dispatches/080410.html
This link leads you to a sound clip where you can learn how computer science is being used to help decide which van Goghs are real and which are fake.

J. BRUCE ISMAY

Hopkinson, Deborah. *Titanic: Voices From the Disaster*. New York: Scholastic Inc., 2012.

Stewart, David. *You Wouldn't Want to Sail on the Titanic!: One Voyage You'd Rather Not Make*. Illustrated by David Antram. Danbury, CT: Franklin Watts, 2001.

http://channel.nationalgeographic.com/channel/titanic-100-years/
This National Geographic site features videos, facts, timelines, and, most important, games about the *Titanic*. Have fun.

JOSEPH JEFFERSON "SHOELESS JOE" JACKSON

Bildner, Phil. *Shoeless Joe and Black Betsy*. Illustrated by C. F. Payne. New York: Simon & Schuster BFYR, 2002.

Elish, Dan. *The Black Sox Scandal of 1919* (Cornerstones of Freedom). Chicago: Children's Press, 2008.

http://ftw.usatoday.com/2013/07/million-dollar-reward-offered-for-missing-document-damning-black-sox/
Recently, sport auctioneers Lelands.com offered a million dollar reward for the signed confession of "Shoeless Joe" Jackson.

AMELIA M. EARHART

Fleming, Candace. *Amelia Lost: The Life and Disappearance of Amelia Earhart*. New York: Schwartz & Wade Books, 2011.

Jerome, Kate Boehm. *Who Was Amelia Earhart?* Illustrated by David Cain and Nancy Harrison. New York: Grosset & Dunlap, 2002.

Stone, Tanya Lee. *Amelia Earhart: A Photographic Story of a Life* (DK Biography). New York: DK Publishing, 2007.

Tanaka, Shelley. *Amelia Earhart: The Legend of the Lost Aviator*. Illustrated by David Craig. New York: Abrams Books for Young Readers, 2008.

http://www.acepilots.com/earhart.html
An exploration of the life and aviation career of one of the world's most famous female pilots.

http://earchives.lib.purdue.edu
This digitized collection features Amelia's personal letters, diaries, maps, and photographs donated by her husband, George Palmer Putnam.

http://tighar.org/
While this site offers background about Amelia's life, the real attraction is the information about her disappearance and the search for her missing plane. You can even watch film footage of her final takeoff from Lae, New Guinea.

INDEX

INDEX

INDEX

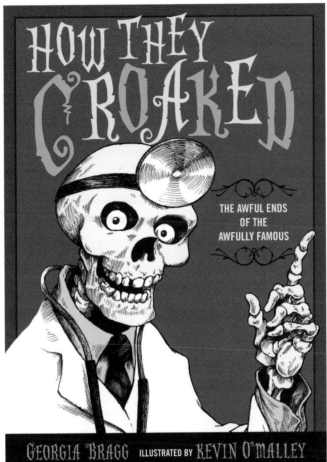

HOW THEY CROAKED

THE AWFUL ENDS OF THE AWFULLY FAMOUS

GEORGIA BRAGG   ILLUSTRATED BY KEVIN O'MALLEY

READ ON for a glimpse into the gory details of the awful deaths of nineteen awfully famous people, including:

Cleopatra

Christopher Columbus

Pocahontas

Galileo Galilei

George Washington

Ludwig van Beethoven

Edgar Allan Poe

Marie Curie

INTRODUCTION

WARNING:
If You Don't Have the Guts for Gore, Do Not Read This Book

REMEMBER WHEN YOU watched *Bambi* for the first time and you got to the part where Bambi's mom dies? And the sweet movie about a family of deer turns into a horror flick? "What the heck was that?" you thought. And in that second you realized that if Bambi's mom can die, so can everybody else.

How They Croaked is like reliving Bambi's mom's death over and over again. Except it's worse because it's the blood, sweat, and guts of real people. In this book are the true stories of how some of the most important people who ever lived—died.

INTRODUCTION

You probably don't know how George Washington, Cleopatra, or Beethoven ate it because every other book you've read skipped over that part. The reason is: getting sick and dying can be a big, ugly mess and, mostly, it's just sad.

There are nice things to say about everybody, but this book is full of bad news. There are funny crying parts and disgusting stupid parts and hideous cool parts, but it's pretty much one train wreck after another. And who can tear their eyes away from a train wreck?

Whether someone had a lung explode or was stabbed to death, died of poison or of a sore throat, there's always someone to blame, fingers to point. Looking back from where we sit now, people a long time ago sure did some dumb stuff—and it's definitely the kind of stuff worth writing about.

Even though everybody in this book has been dead a long time, reading about their last dying days will make your toes curl. But these stories will also fascinate you and make you realize how lucky you are to live in a world with painkillers and X-rays and soap and 911.

Who knows, maybe people in the future will look back at us and wonder, what the heck were *they* thinking? So here's a warning: take care of yourself, the world, and everybody in it. But if you don't have the guts for gore, DO NOT READ THIS BOOK.

KING TUT

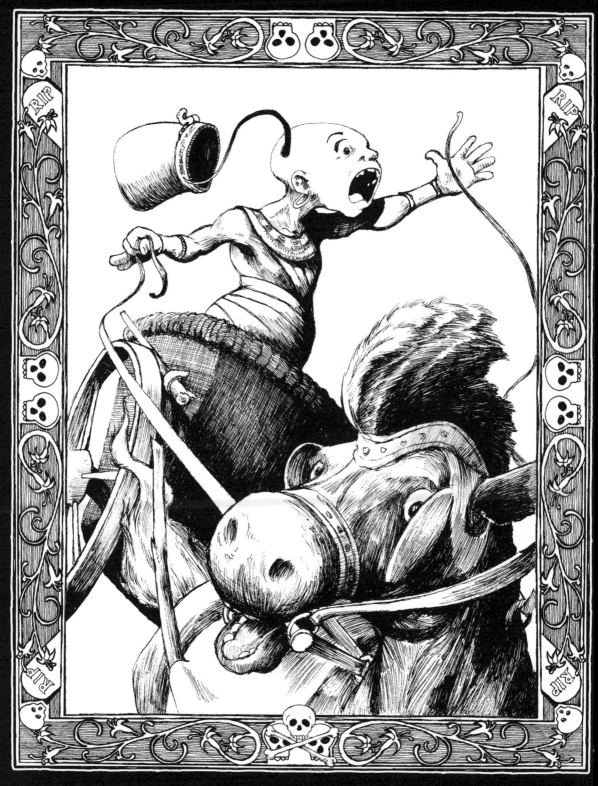

BACK UP
THE U-HAUL

King of Egypt
Born: Egypt,
circa 1342 BC
Died: Egypt,
1323 BC
19 years old

KING TUT IS more famous for being dead than alive. He was a blip in Egyptian history until 1922, when some explorers hit pay dirt and found his three-thousand-year-old mummy nestled inside a giant sarcophagus. That sounds like a human body part, but it's just a fancy word meaning a stone box for a dead body. These grave-robbing explorers broke into Tut's tomb and took all his gold. And there was a lot of it because King Tut definitely planned on being king in the afterlife. What he didn't plan on was being probed, sliced, dismembered, X-rayed, scanned, and drilled for his DNA.

Pictures of a bird, two hooks, a comb, an arrow, a sandal strap, and a couple of speed bumps spell Tutankhamun in hieroglyphics. Today, we just call him King Tut. He is also called the Boy King. He got to be the king of Egypt when he was nine years old. He was only ten when he married Ankhsenamun, who unfortunately was his half sister, which was okay back then but would be really wrong now. Besides ruling Egypt, Tut did regular kid things like riding in chariots, throwing sticks, and firing his slingshot.

And then, *poof*, he died.

Even though Tut had died, he wasn't finished. Ancient Egyptians believed there is a life after this one, so after his death Tut's corpse was prepped for life number two. He was given the seventy-day royal mummy treatment.

So that Tut wouldn't rot on the trip to the next life, the embalmers scooped his insides out from top to bottom. To get his brains out, a long bronze needle with a hook on the end was shoved up his nose. His brain was broken up into teeny bits and pulled out one piece at a time. The Egyptians believed the brain's only job was to keep the ears apart, and that the heart did all the thinking.

They didn't take Tut's teeth, nails, and eyeballs. They left Tut's heart in his body because he was going to need that to think. And they left his genitals so no one would mistake him for Queen Tut.

Next, they cut open Tut's stomach and pulled out whatever they could get their hands on—like his liver, stomach, lungs, and twenty-two feet of intestines. Everything was washed, dried, put into four jars, and wrapped to go with him.

They covered Tut's altered corpse with natron (saltlike stuff) and put it on a slanted board with grooves in it so his bodily fluids flowed directly into a tub at the end. His gutted body was completely dried, which was especially difficult considering the human body is 75 percent water. They stuffed his chest with wads of cloth to soak up the inside juice. Every weensy drop of blood, rag, and leftover bit of Tut was saved and crammed into big jars for him to take along for his next excellent adventure.

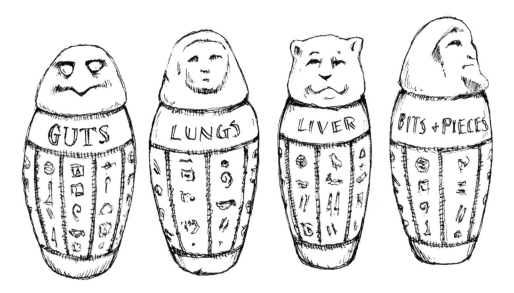

Tut's cadaver gave new meaning to the words "stiff" and "stinky," so it was smeared with scented goo to make it smell better and to make it feel less like Tut jerky.

Then, to make him look like a real mummy and to keep him from falling apart during a ceremony when a priest stood him up and offered him grapes, Tut's pruned corpse was encased by half a football field worth of fabric strips spun around his body like cotton candy, along with 143 charms woven in for good luck. To seal everything, they poured warmed plant resin (sap) all over Tut's wrapped body. Think superglue.

Meanwhile, servants picked up a few of his kingly things from the palace, including a couple of thrones, two slingshots, two jars of honey, six chariots, thirty golden statues, thirty-five model boats, 130 walking sticks, 427 arrows, and lots of sandals.

When Tut died, no one in Egypt had built a pyramid for a dead king for two hundred years because tomb raiders had trashed every single one of them, taking everything—including the mummies. Tomb raiders took off with the mother lode of ancient Egyptian history.

So they buried Tut in a tomb hidden under a sand dune in the middle of the desert known as the Valley of the Kings.

And there he rested undisturbed for three thousand years.

In 1922, Howard Carter—an English guy who had been digging around the Valley for twenty years—found Tut's intact tomb under a trillion grains of sand. Carter took ten years to pick through Tut's personal things and divvy them up to museums all over the world. The Egyptians told Carter, "Go home already."

But first Carter and his team did an "autopsy." It was hard to do because Tut was superglued to the bottom of his coffin, and his famous gold mask was attached to his head. Carter managed to figure out Tut had been a teenager when he died because his teeth hadn't all come in yet and his leg bones weren't fully developed.

King Tut was returned to his sarcophagus and went nighty-night back in his tomb in the Valley of the Kings for about forty more years.

In 1968, experts X-rayed Tut's mummy to figure out how he had died. They noticed Tut's breastbone, genitals, one thumb, and a few ribs were missing. The X-rays also showed that his vertebrae were fused together and his skull was misshapen. They analyzed the facts and announced, "King Tut was murdered!"

Historians took the murder theory and fit the facts to the crime. Egyptologists had a new angle, history books were rewritten, and museum exhibits were revamped.

Tut stayed put for ten more years, until scientists removed him from his stone box again in 1978. He was still dead. They took more X-rays but never published their findings. And from a bone sample, they analyzed his blood. Tut's blood types were A2 and MN.

In 2005, there was new equipment to try out on Tut: a CT scan (way better than an X-ray). That was the first time anyone got a good look at what Carter forgot to mention after his so-called autopsy. He had broken off Tut's arms and legs and sliced Tut's chest down the middle. Carter also chiseled Tut's head off to get it free of the solid-gold mask. And to get Tut's 143 good-luck charms, Carter cut the body wrapping with an X-Acto blade. Afterward he glued Tut back together with wax and put the mangled mummy in a bed of sand. He didn't bother to reattach Tut's genitals, thumb, and ribs; he just buried them in the sand. And then he put Tut back inside the coffin.

Carter was just another tomb raider after all.

The CT scan showed that Tut had an overbite, a small cleft palate, and a bend in his spine. But there was something else: Tut had a broken leg, and this one was not Carter's doing.

The Boy King got a new obit—"Tut died of a broken leg that got infected." He went back into his stone box—but not for long.

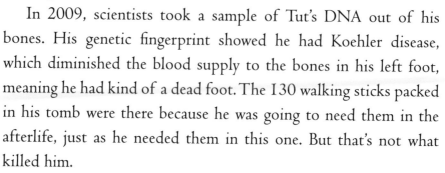

In 2009, scientists took a sample of Tut's DNA out of his bones. His genetic fingerprint showed he had Koehler disease, which diminished the blood supply to the bones in his left foot, meaning he had kind of a dead foot. The 130 walking sticks packed in his tomb were there because he was going to need them in the afterlife, just as he needed them in this one. But that's not what killed him.

Tut had malaria, a disease you get after being bitten by an infected mosquito. Malaria, along with his broken leg and dead foot, made for a dead king.

He died in 1323 BC. He was only nineteen years old. It didn't take a CT scan to see that Tut's leg was broken; it was visible to the naked eye and mentioned in Carter's original autopsy. It was also noted that Tut had a scabby, discolored indentation on the left side of his face. At the time, no one really knew what a three-thousand-year-old insect bite might look like, but now that we know Tut died of malaria, that scab on his face could be the mosquito bite that eventually killed him.

Tut's mummy is back in his tomb. Maybe now he can rest in peace. But for how long?

THINGS TO DO WITH OLD MUMMIES

PHARAOHS AND MILLIONS OF COMMON people were mummified in ancient times. Later, mummies were shipped by the ton all over the world for other uses, including:

1. MUMMY MEDICINE

For hundreds of years (1300–1800) doctors believed burned and pulverized mummies made into oils and powders could cure:

abscesses	paralysis
coughs	poisoning
epilepsy	rashes
fractures	ulcers
palpitations	

SIDE EFFECTS OF SWALLOWING MUMMY MEDICINE
- serious vomiting
- evil-smelling breath

2. MUMMY PAPER

Every mummy has at least thirty pounds of cloth around it. Used mummy cloth was made into brown butcher paper in the mid-1800s for packaging meat (unbeknownst to shoppers). But fairly soon, mummy paper was discontinued—after an outbreak of cholera among the workers at the paper mill.

3. MUMMY PAINT

Ground-up mummy produced a deep brown favored by Romantic painters (1790–1850). There were problems with this paint:

- It never dried.
- It dripped down the painting in hot weather.
- It contracted and cracked in cold weather.
- It ruined any color under, over, or near it.

MUMMY EYEBALLS

MUMMY EYE SOCKETS LOOK EMPTY, but they're not. Eyeballs shrink to almost nothing during the drying process. The empty-looking sockets were sometimes filled with cloth, onions, or stones and painted to look like eyeballs.

COOL FACT

If mummy eyeballs are rehydrated, they return to almost normal size.

KING TUT UNDER GLASS

TUT'S MUMMY WAS REMOVED FROM its sarcophagus and placed in a climate-controlled glass case in Tut's tomb, which was open for viewing for the first time in 2007. The mummy has been examined five times in the past, but only now is the public able to view it.

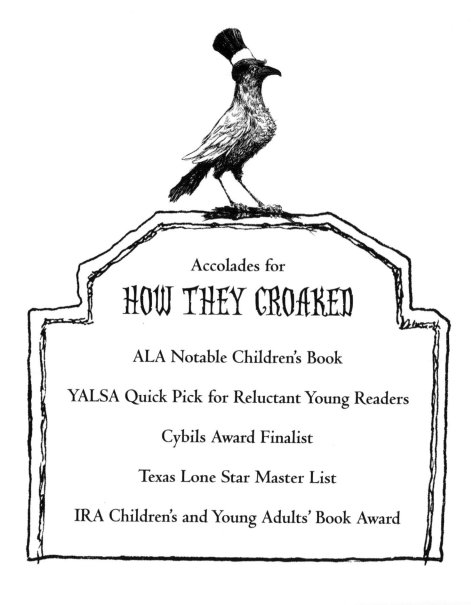

Accolades for

HOW THEY CROAKED

ALA Notable Children's Book

YALSA Quick Pick for Reluctant Young Readers

Cybils Award Finalist

Texas Lone Star Master List

IRA Children's and Young Adults' Book Award

GEORGIA BRAGG

is the author of *How They Croaked*, as well as *Matisse on the Loose*, a middle-grade novel. She was a printmaker, painter, and storyboard artist before becoming a writer. Georgia lives in Los Angeles with her husband, two children, and two cats.

www.georgiabragg.com

KEVIN O'MALLEY

is the illustrator of *How They Croaked*, the coauthor and illustrator of the popular Miss Malarkey series, and the author/illustrator of the *New York Times* bestseller *Gimme Cracked Corn and I Will Share* and many other books for children. He lives in Maryland.

www.booksbyomalley.com